Real World
Colouring Book
For Advanced Users & Adults

50 Images

**Created From Real Life Photos
For You To Colour As You Please.**

ISBN 978-0-359-97209-8
90000
9 780359 972098

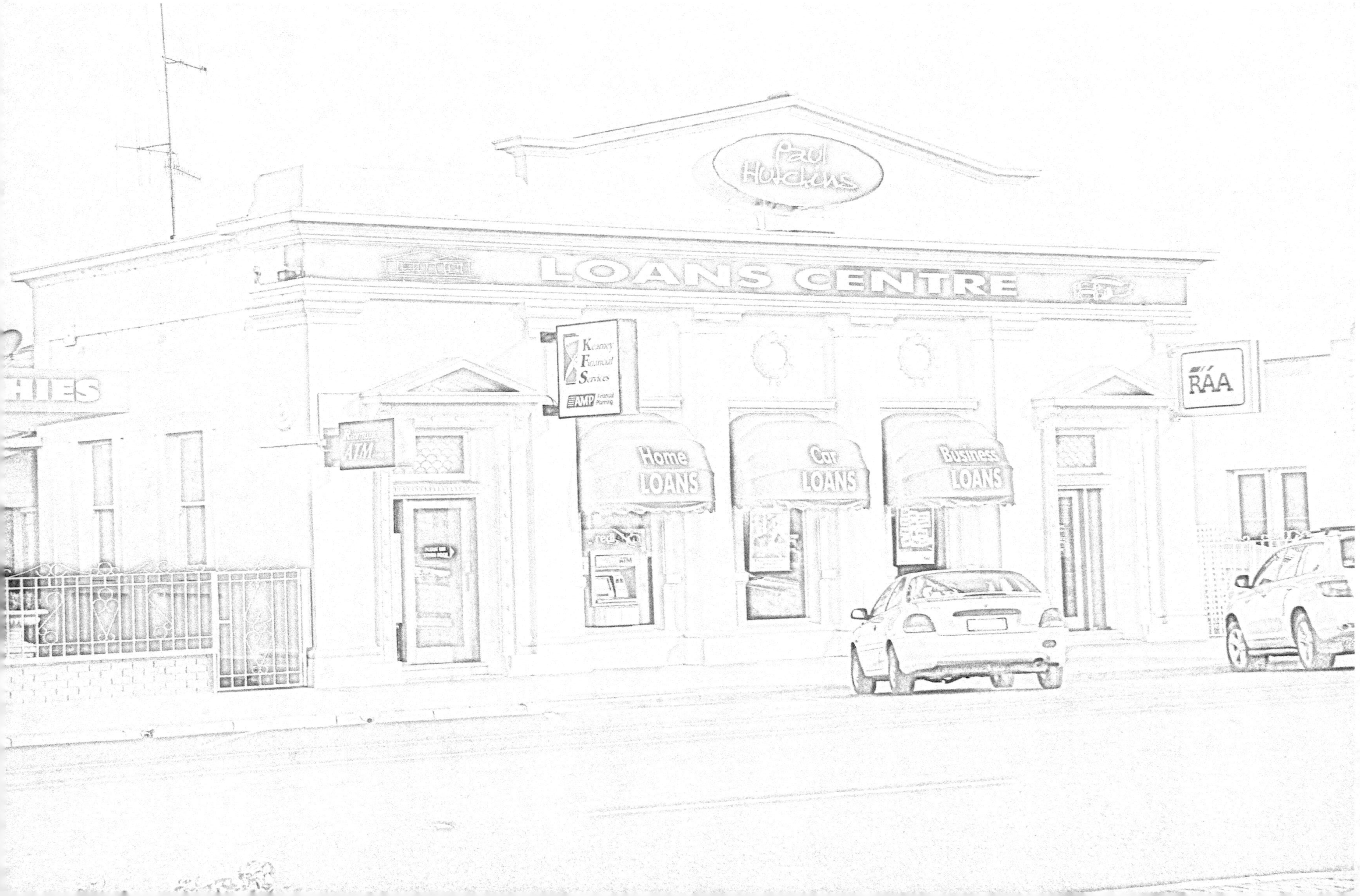
Paul Hotchkins
LOANS CENTRE
Kearney Financial Services
AMP Financial Planning
RAA
ATM
Home LOANS
Car LOANS
Business LOANS
HIES

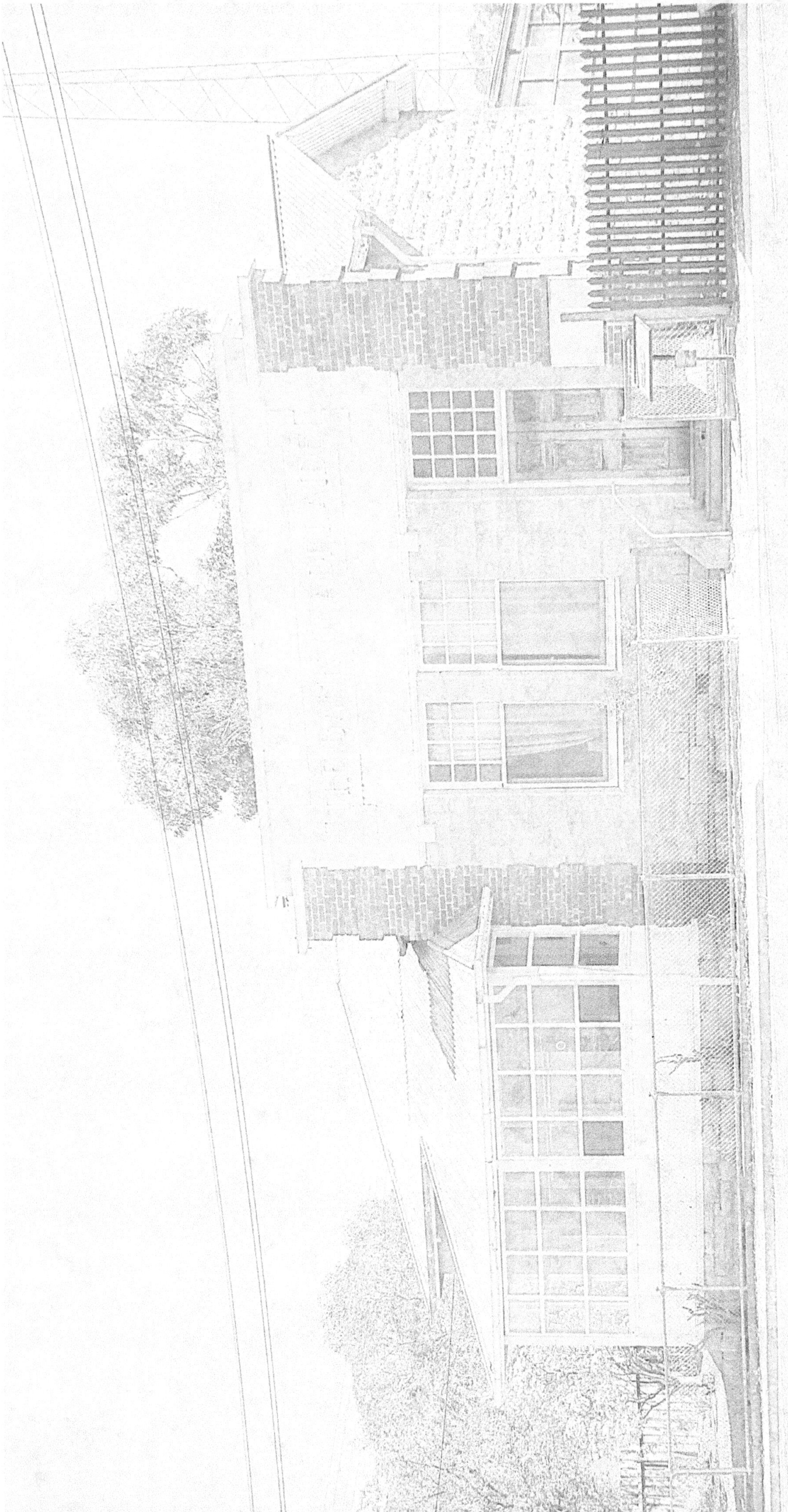

TAKE AWAY FOOD PIZZA BAR
ICE,SOUVENIRS,DRINKS
Morgan Riverview Cafe

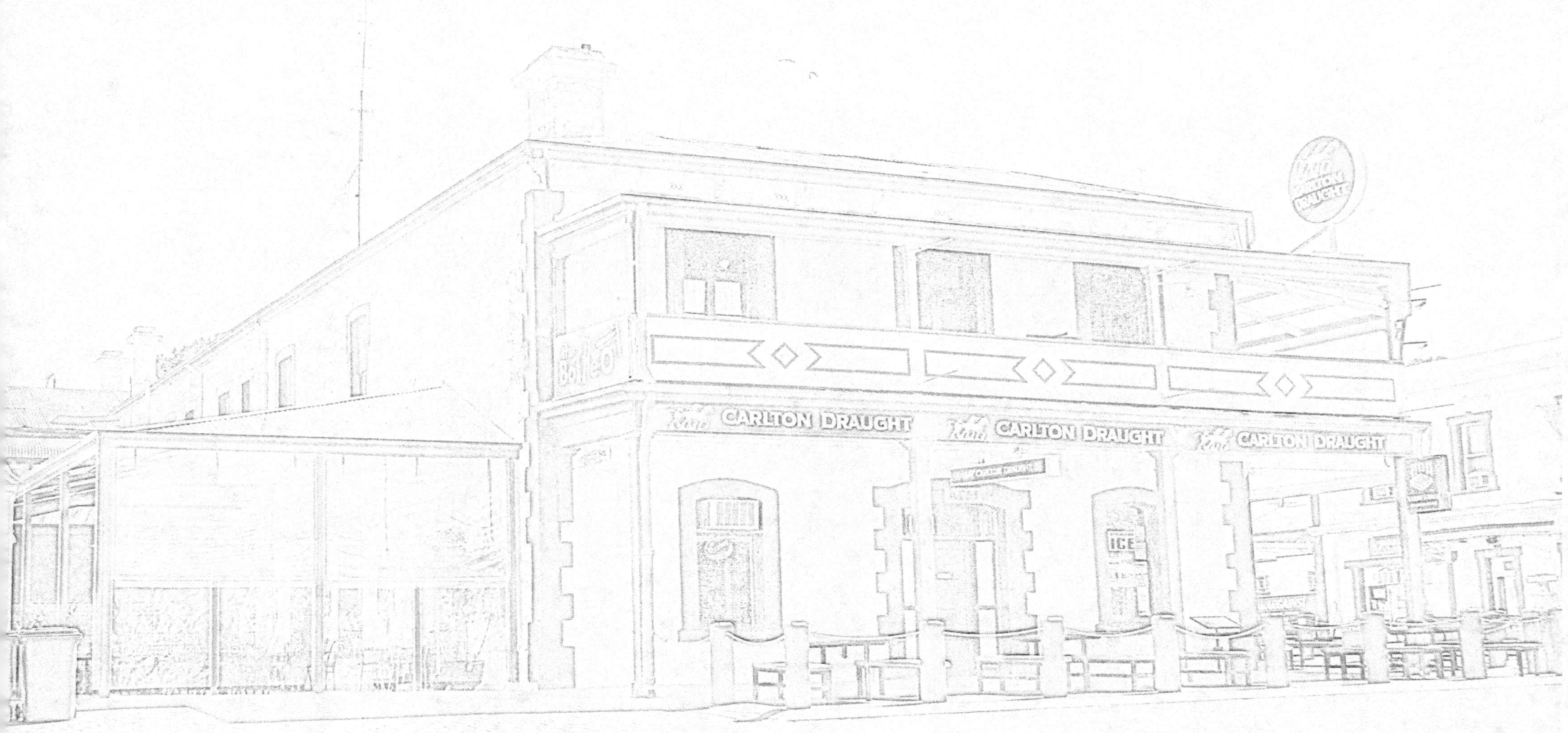
CARLTON DRAUGHT
CARLTON DRAUGHT
CARLTON DRAUGHT
ICE

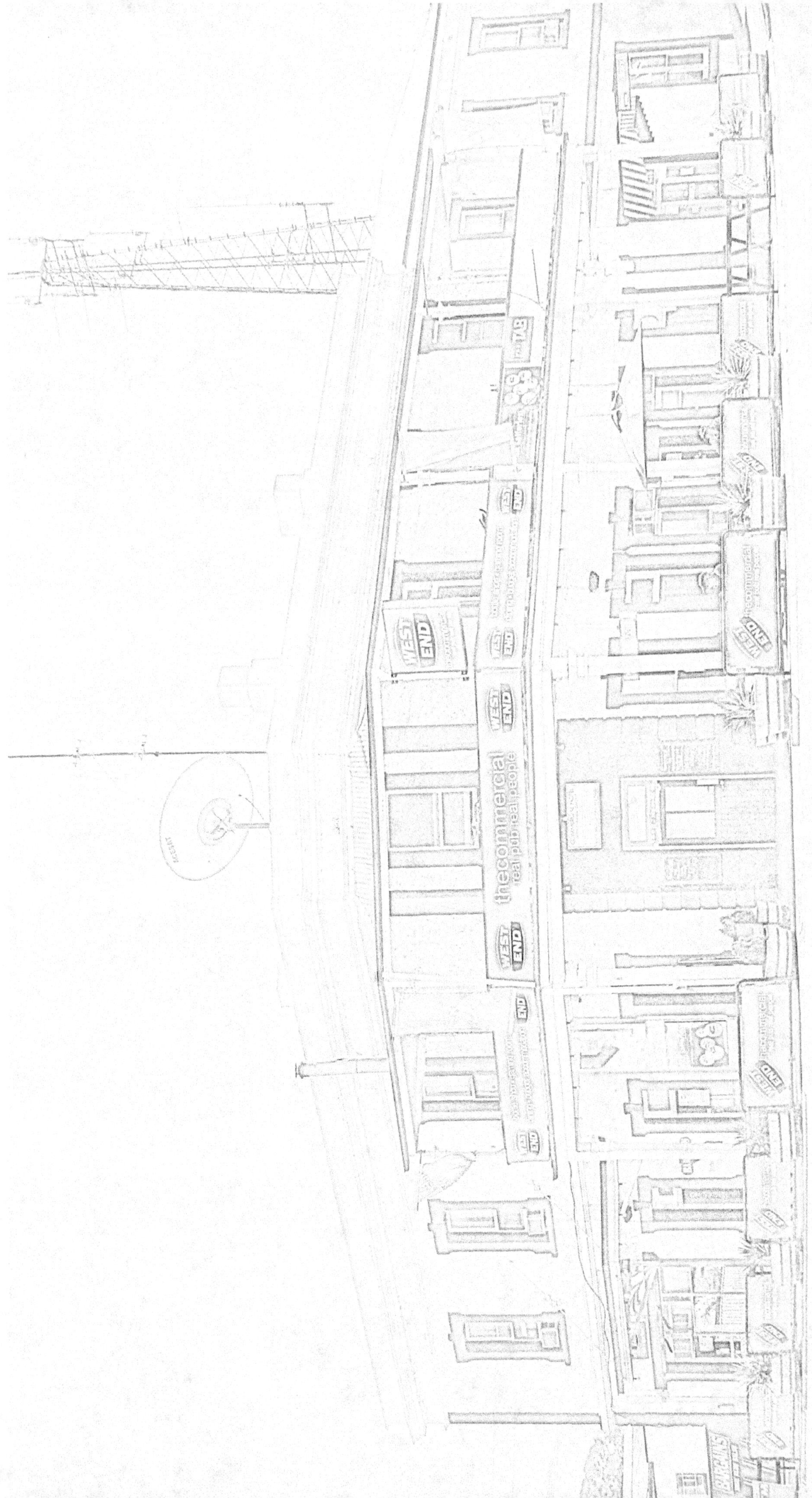
thecommercial
real pub real people
WEST END

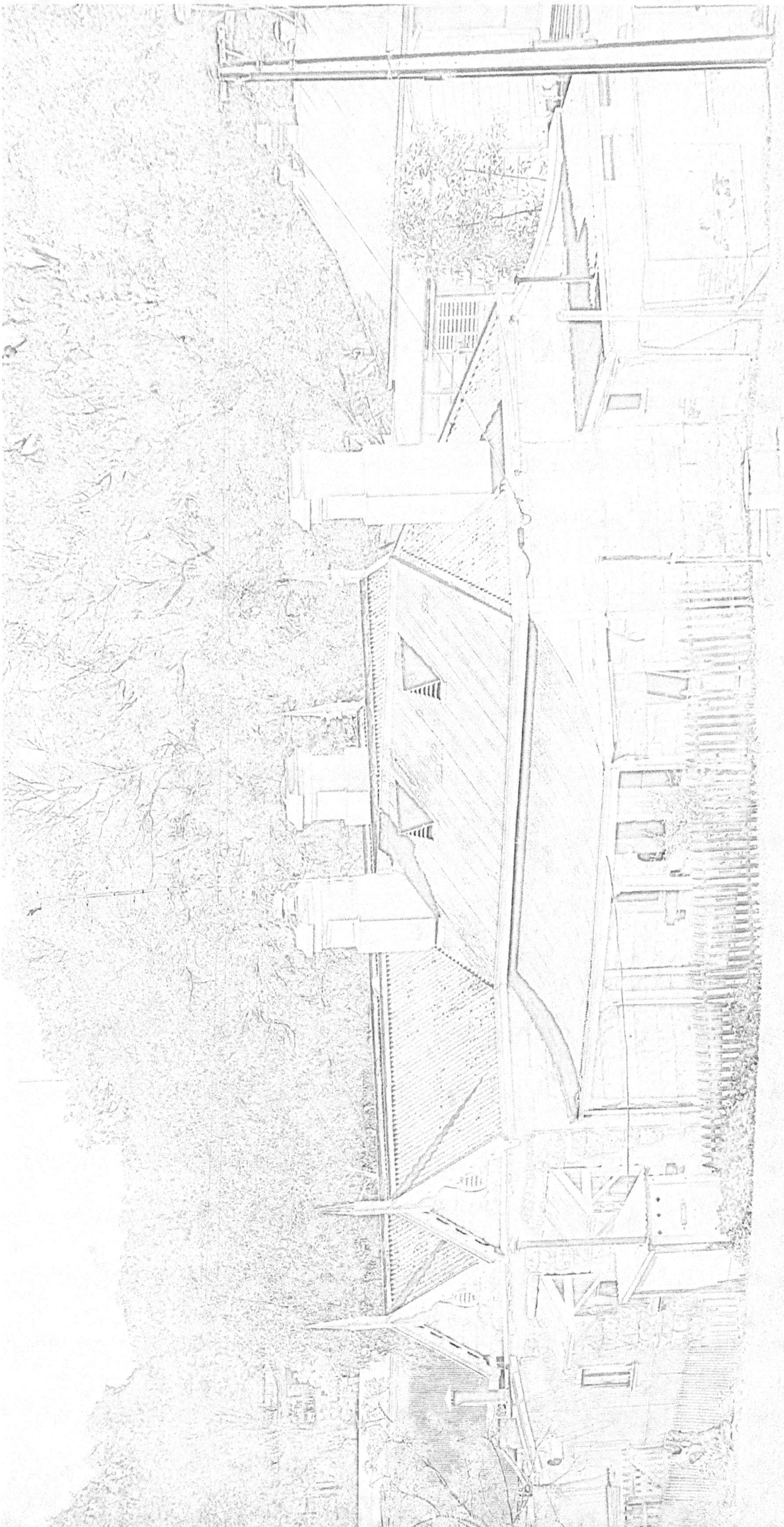

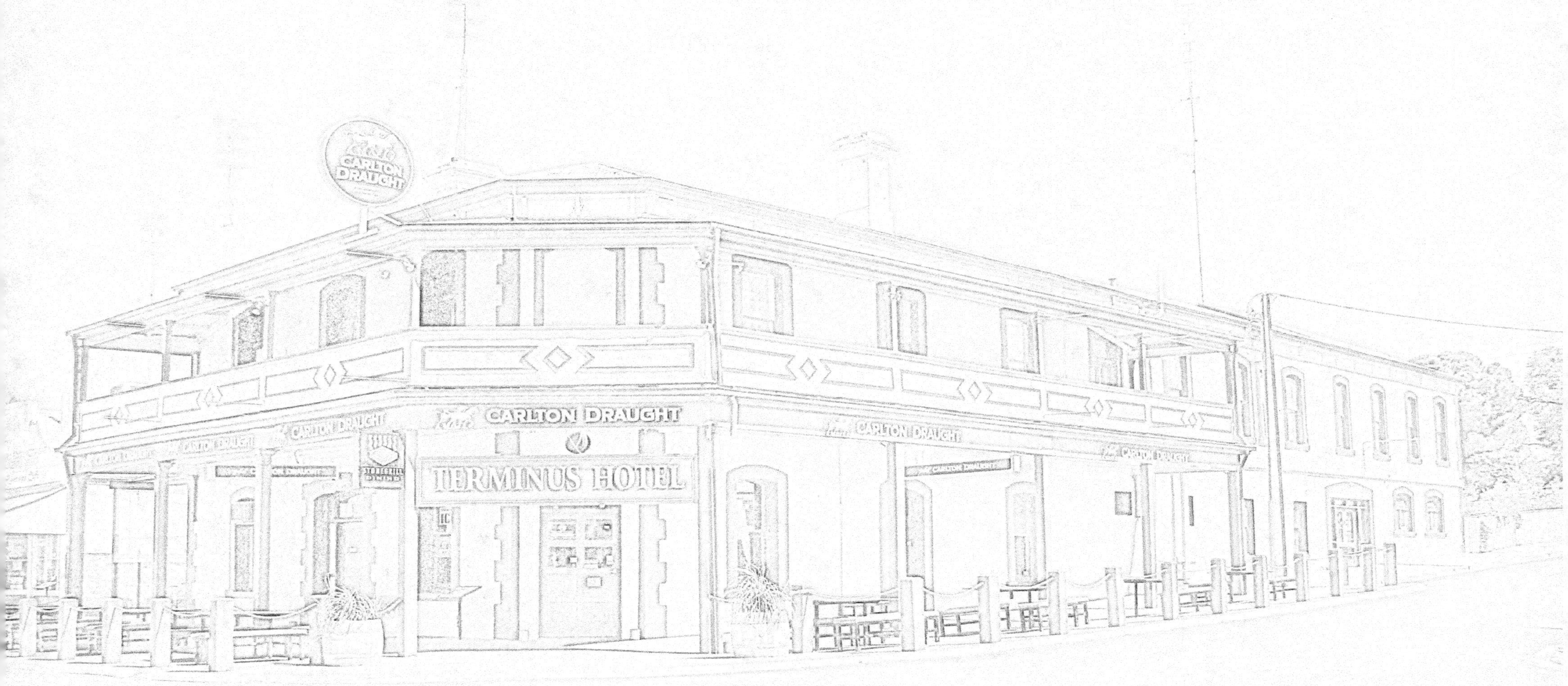
CARLTON DRAUGHT
CARLTON DRAUGHT
TERMINUS HOTEL
CARLTON DRAUGHT
CARLTON DRAUGHT
CARLTON DRAUGHT
CARLTON DRAUGHT

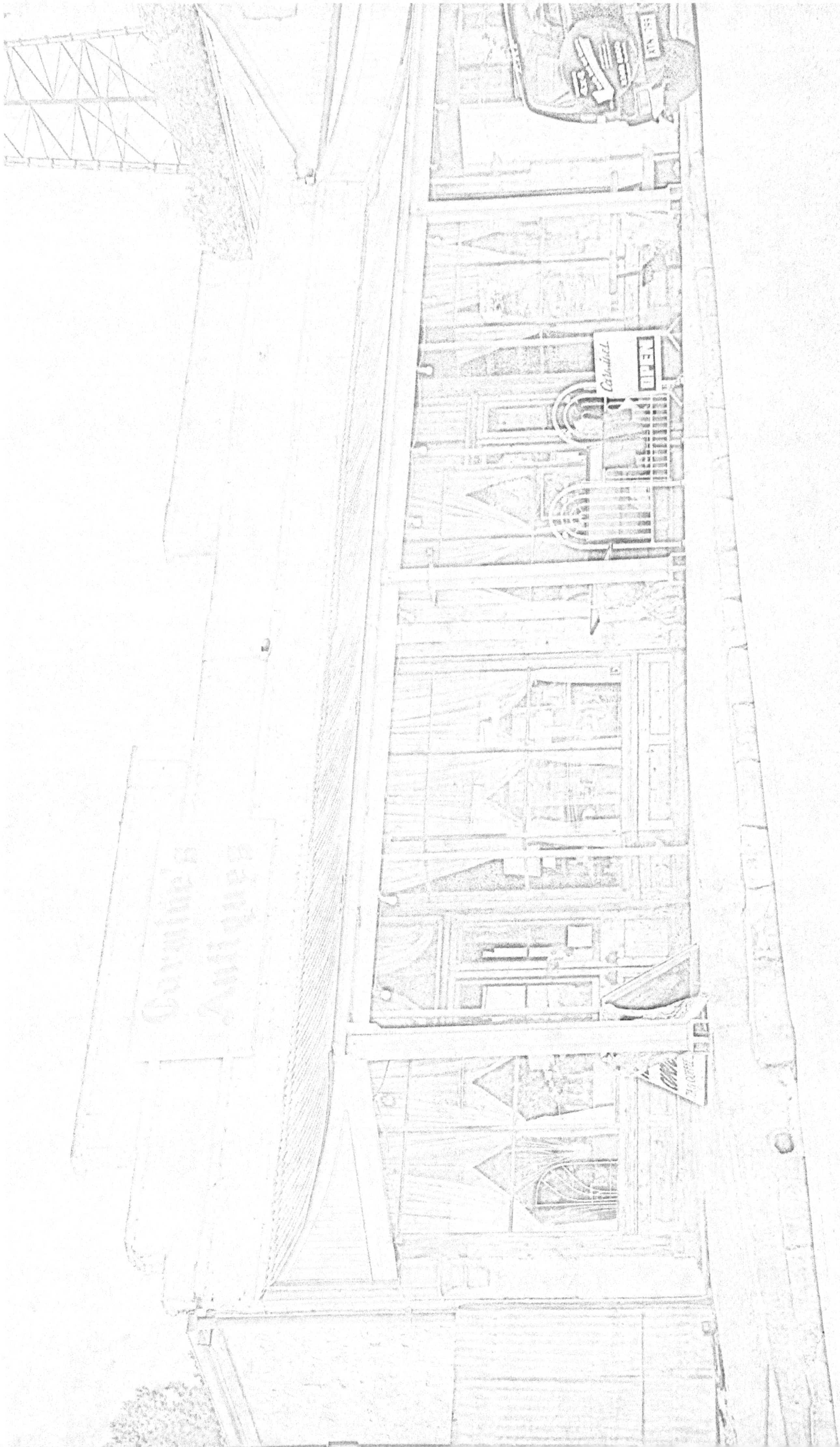

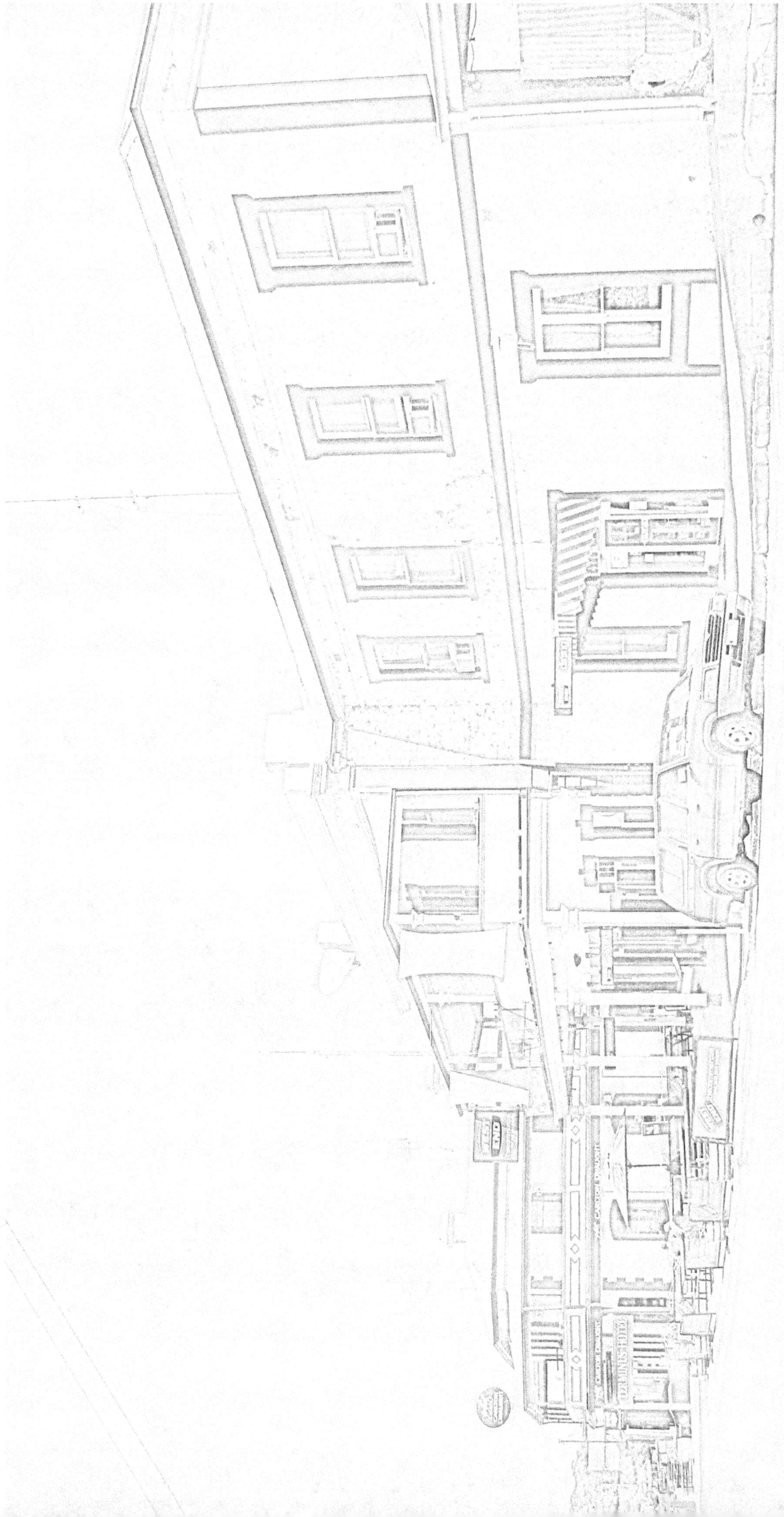

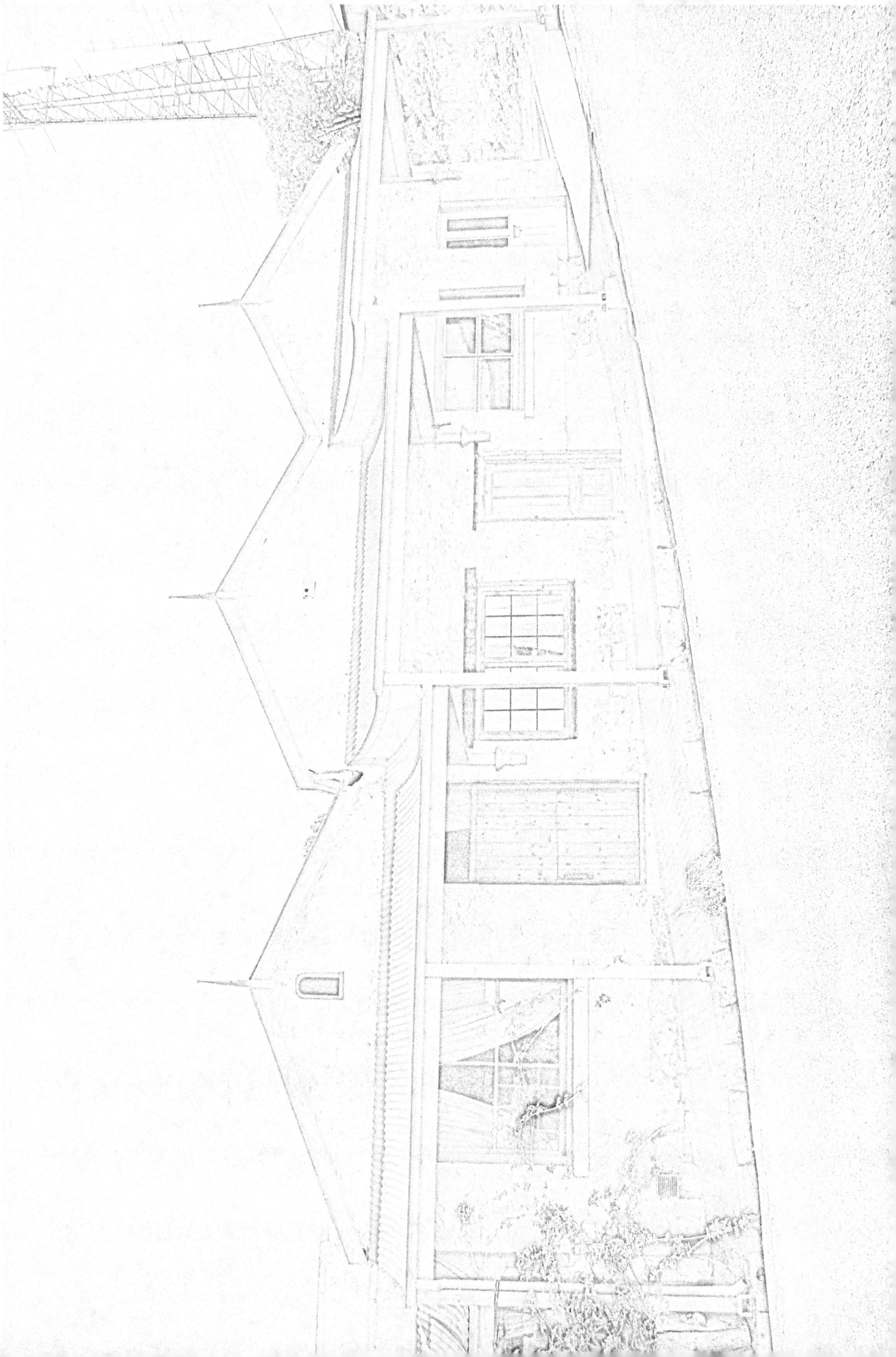

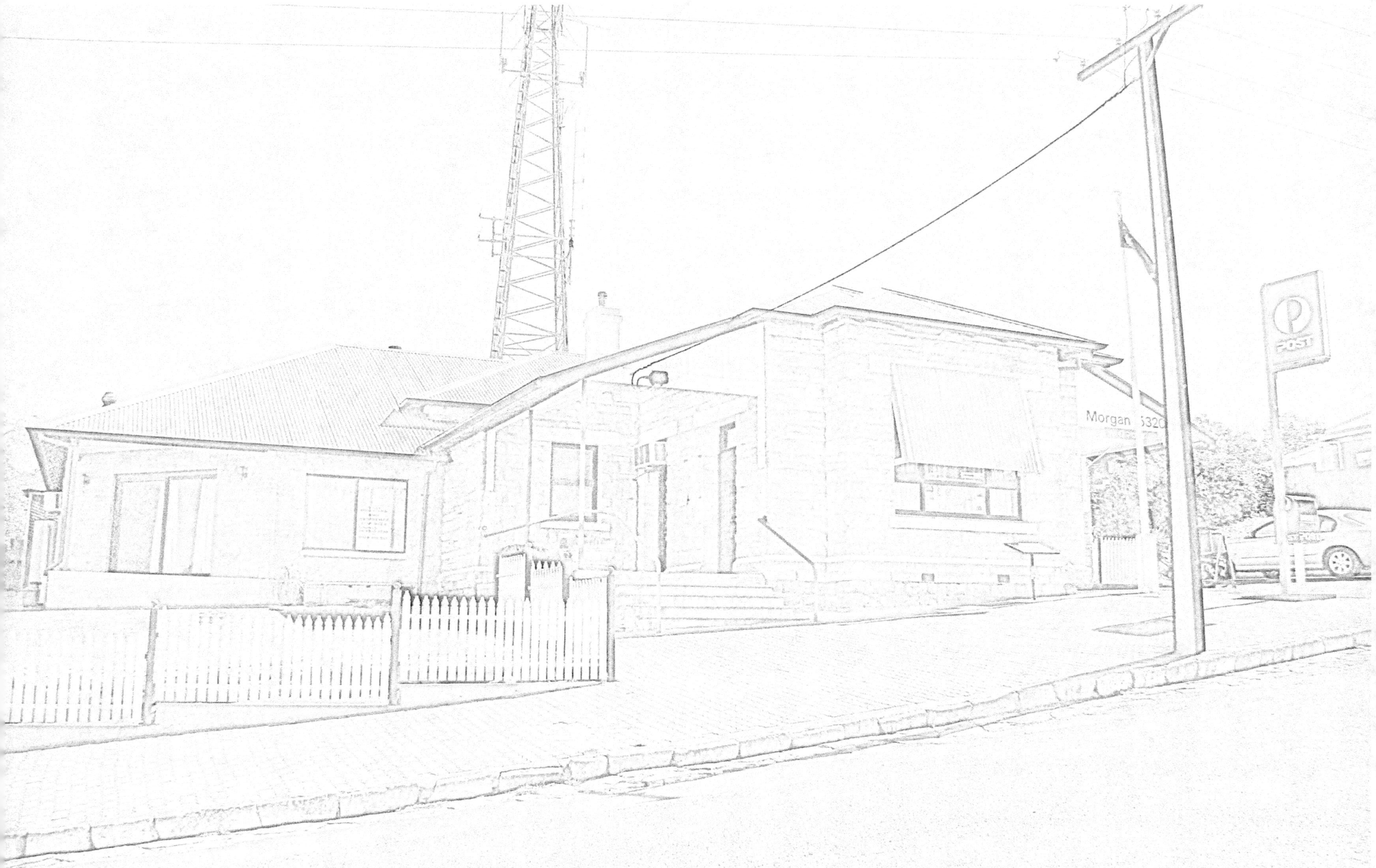
POST
Morgan

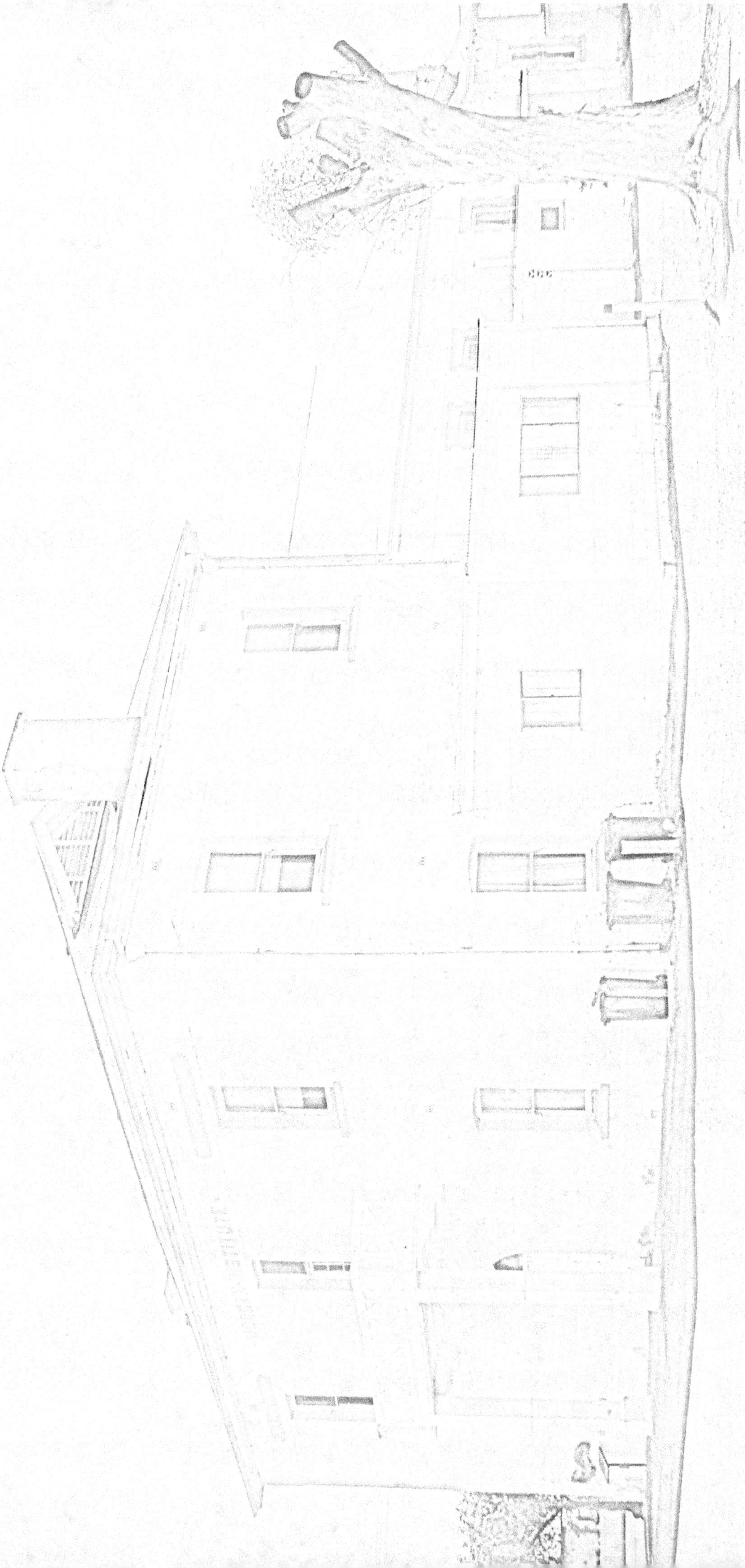

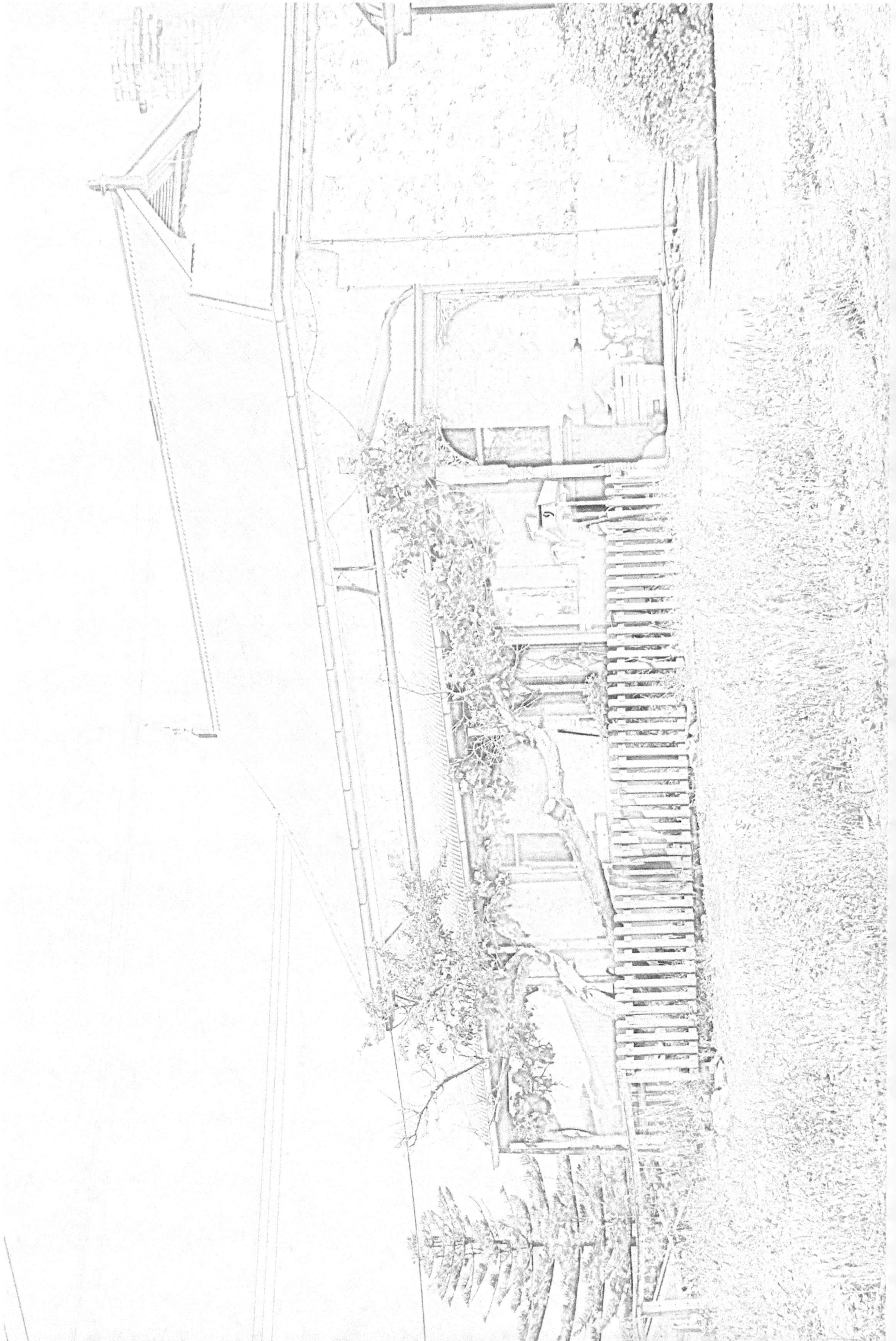

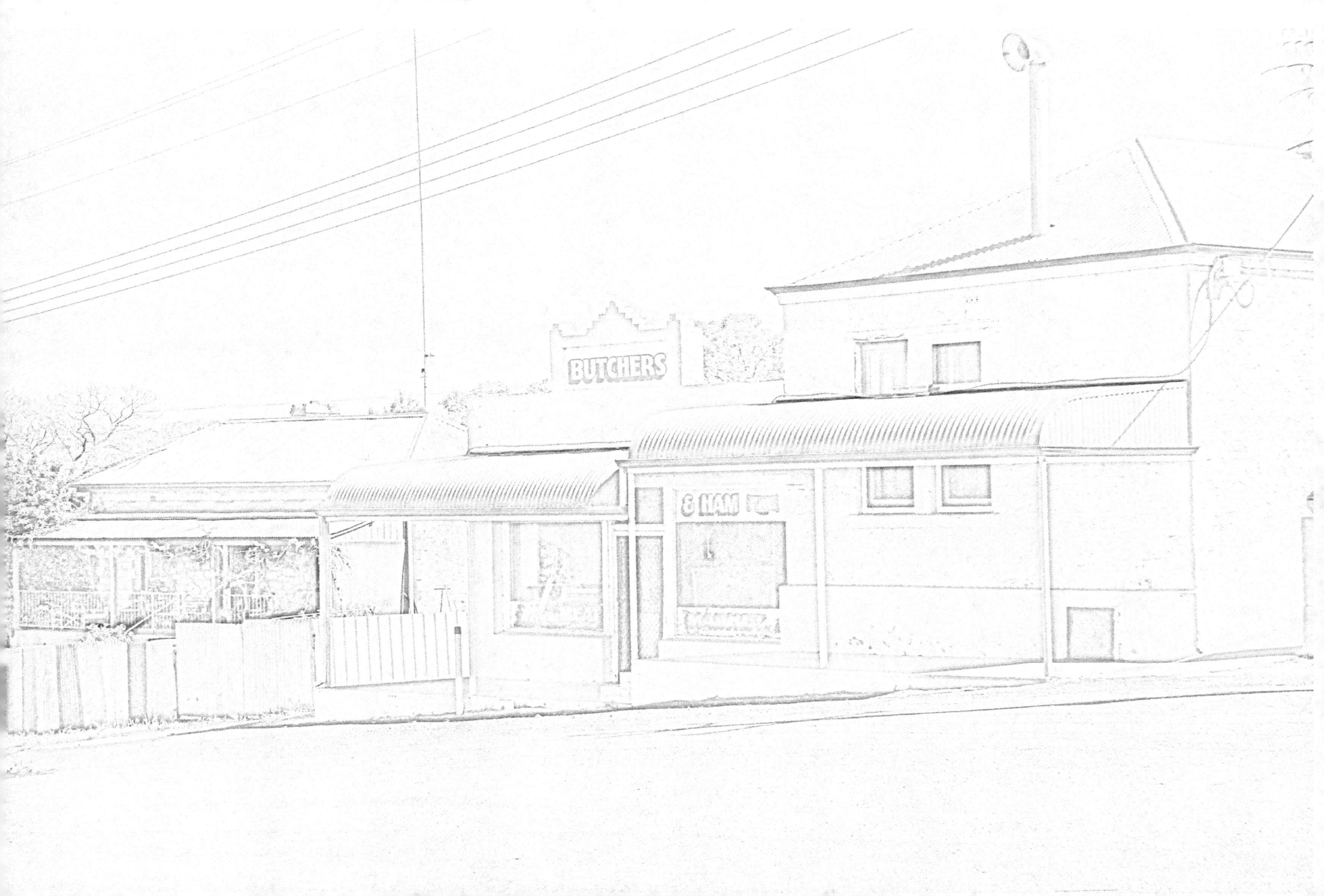
BUTCHERS
& HAM

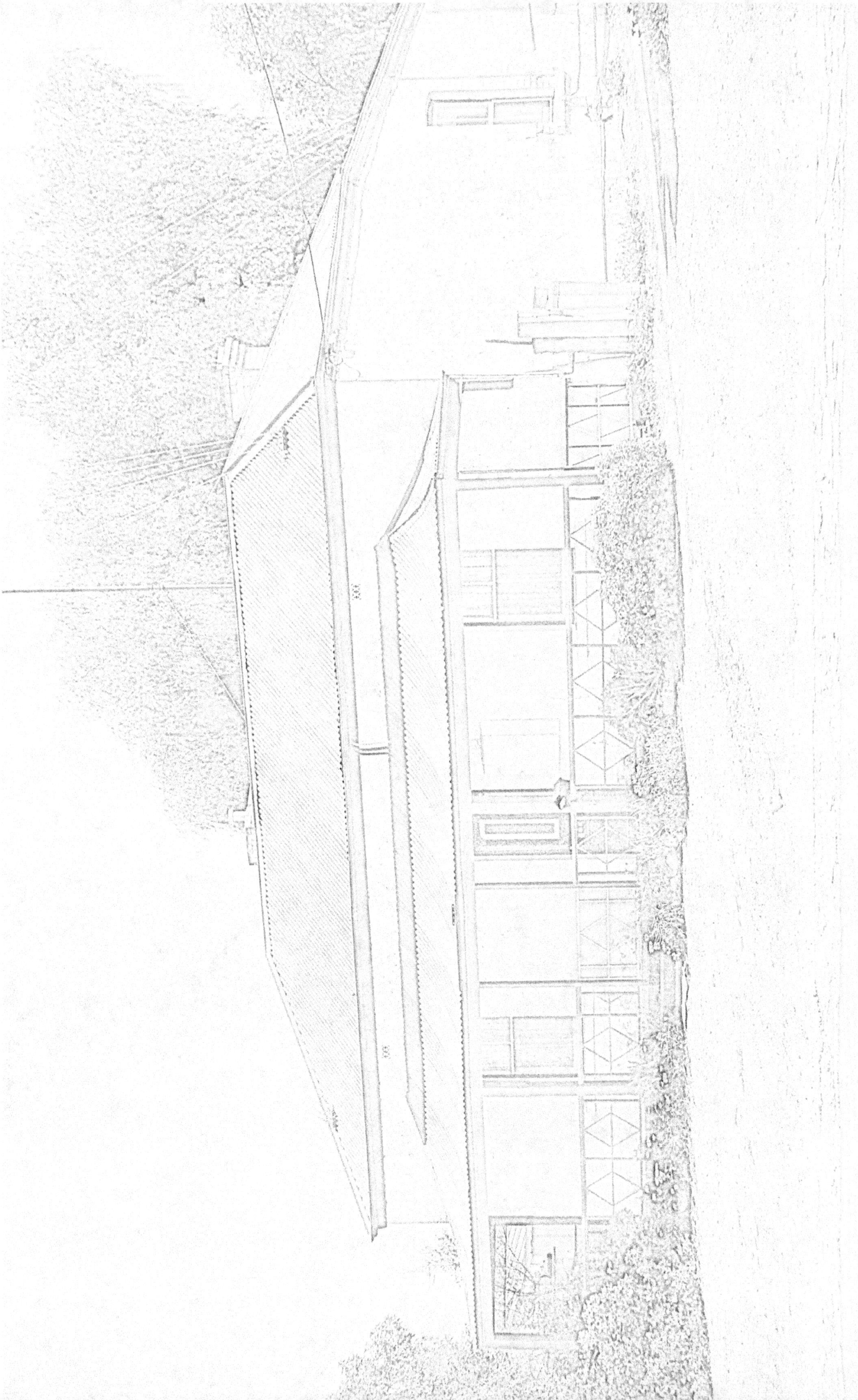

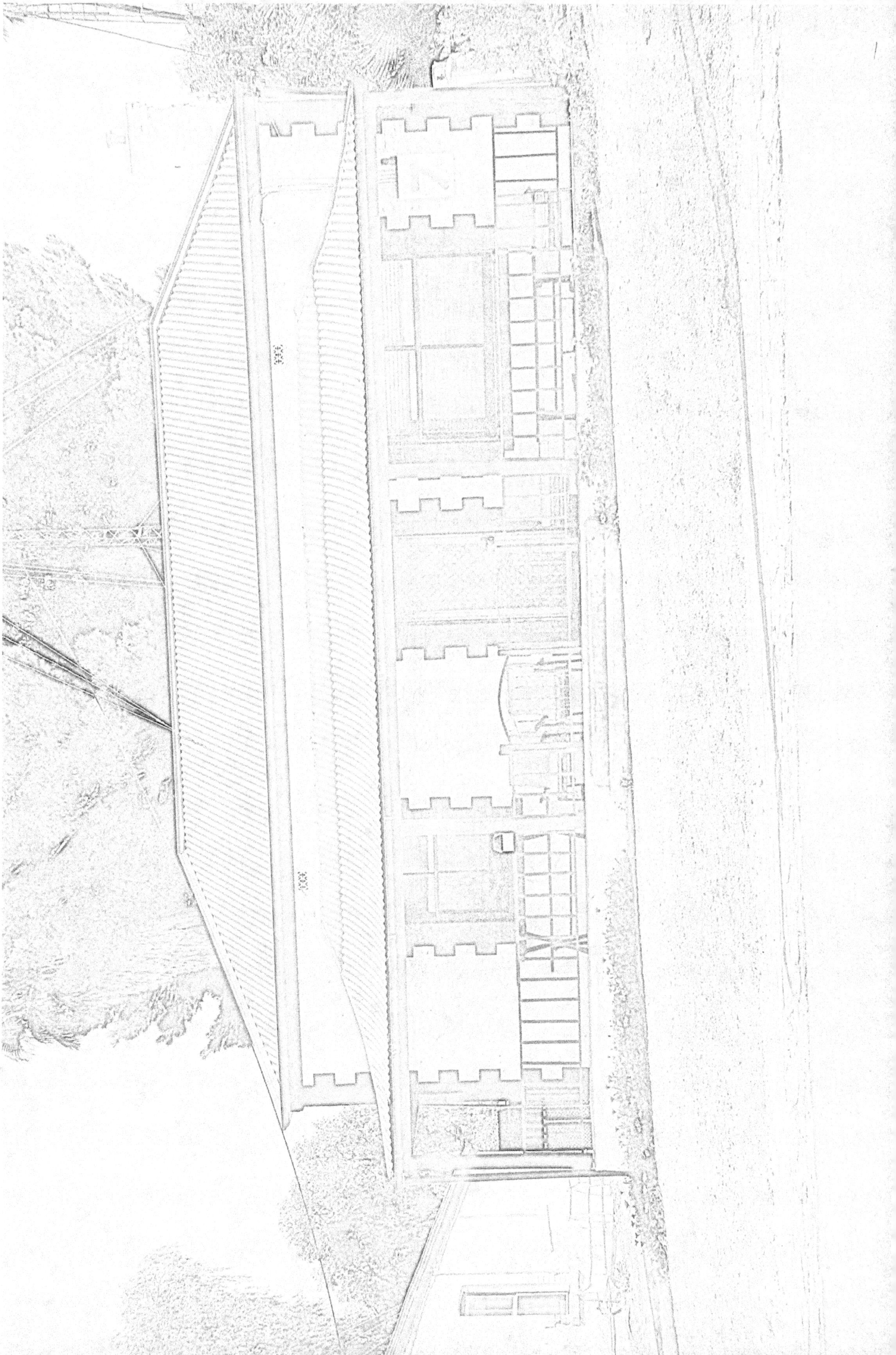

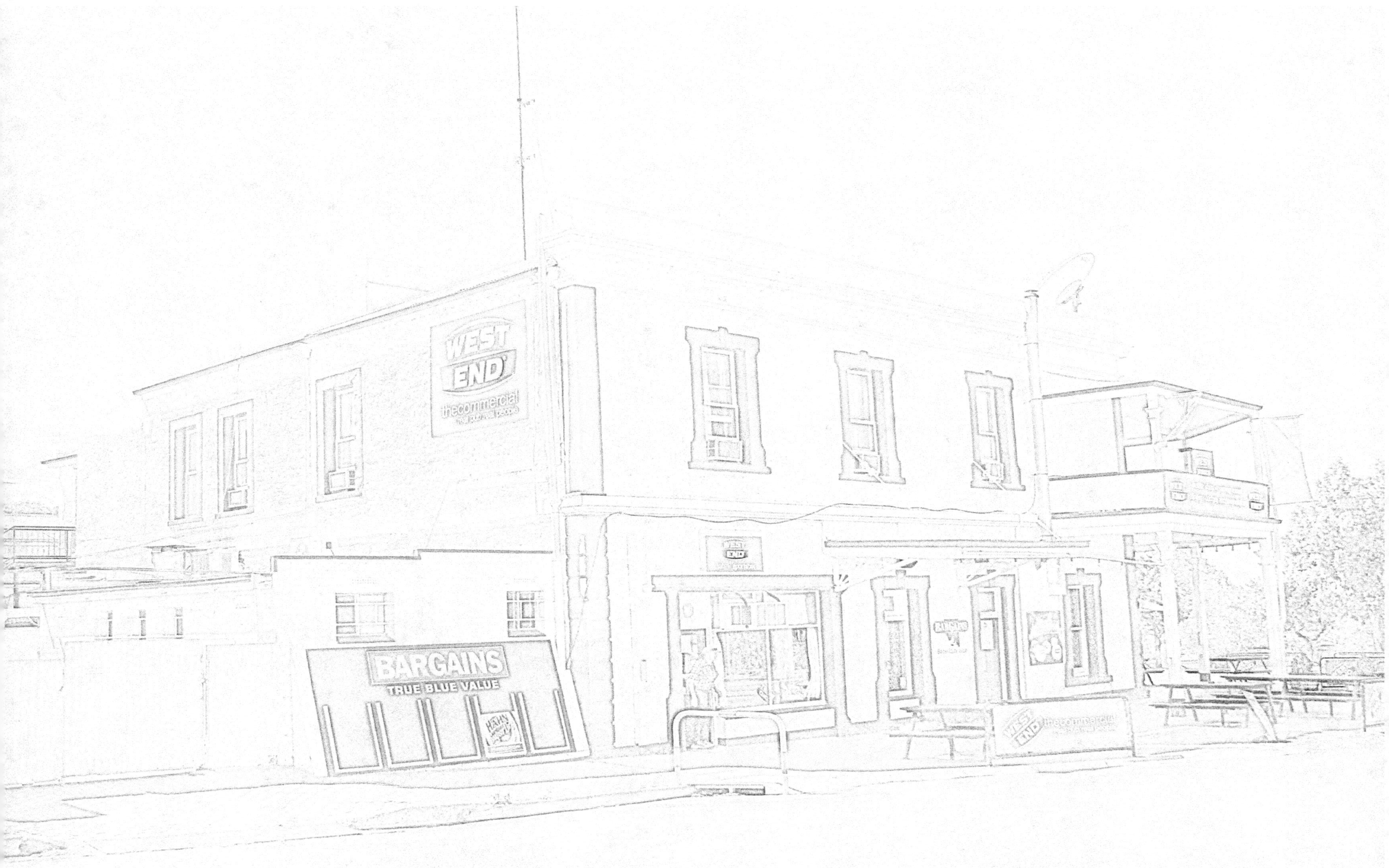
WEST
END
thecommercial
BARGAINS
TRUE BLUE VALUE
WEST
END
thecommercial

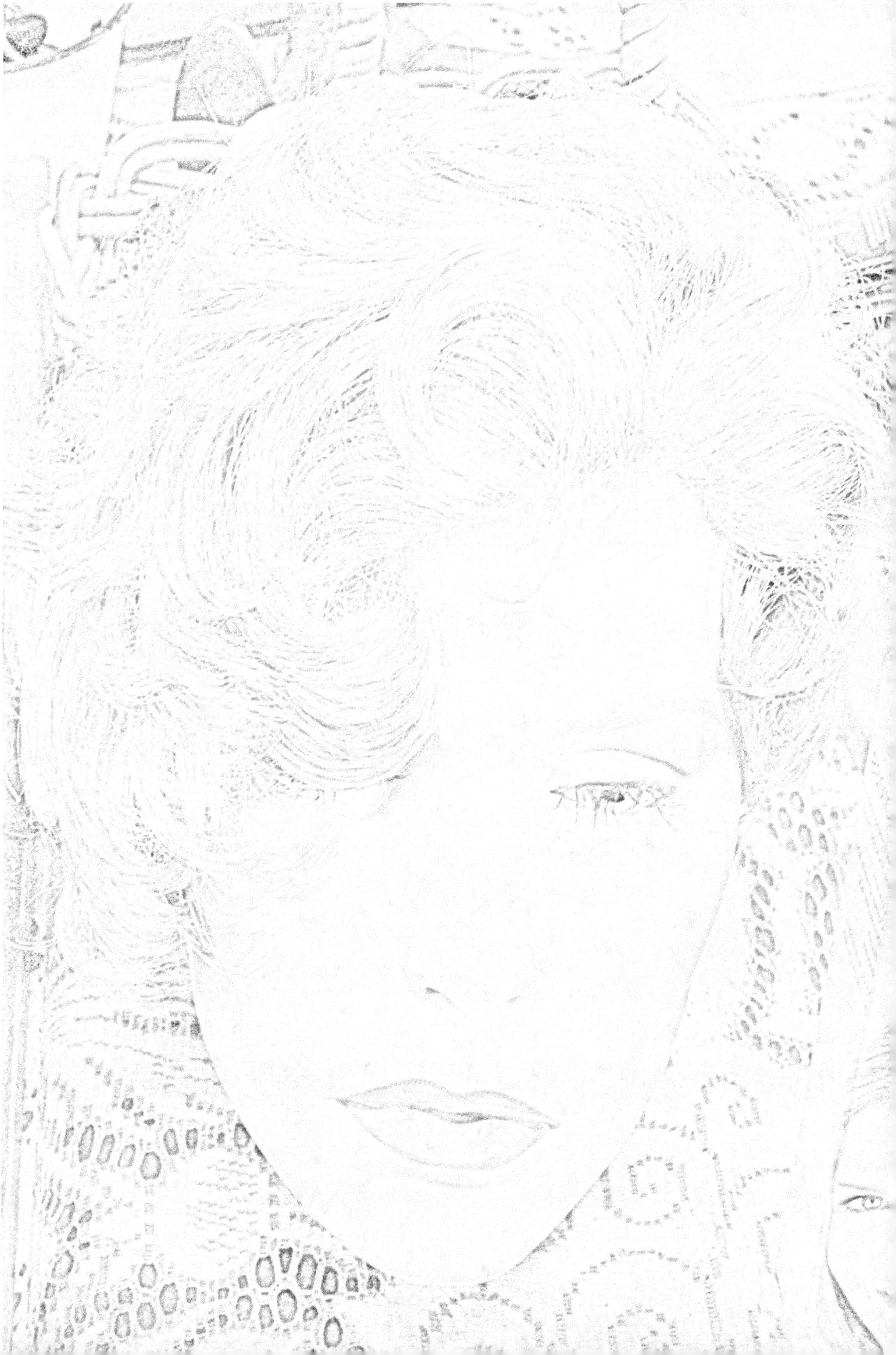

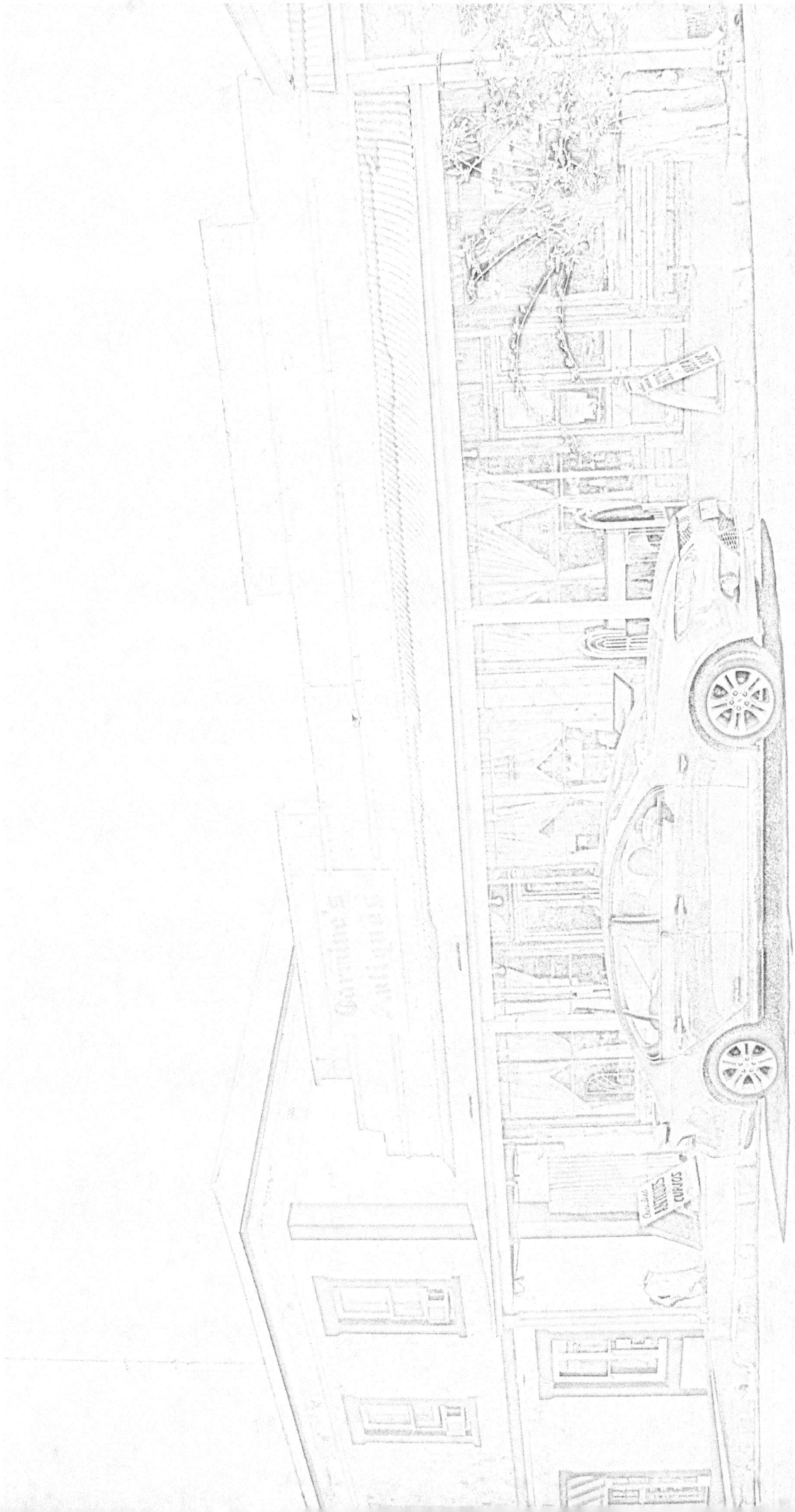
CURIOS

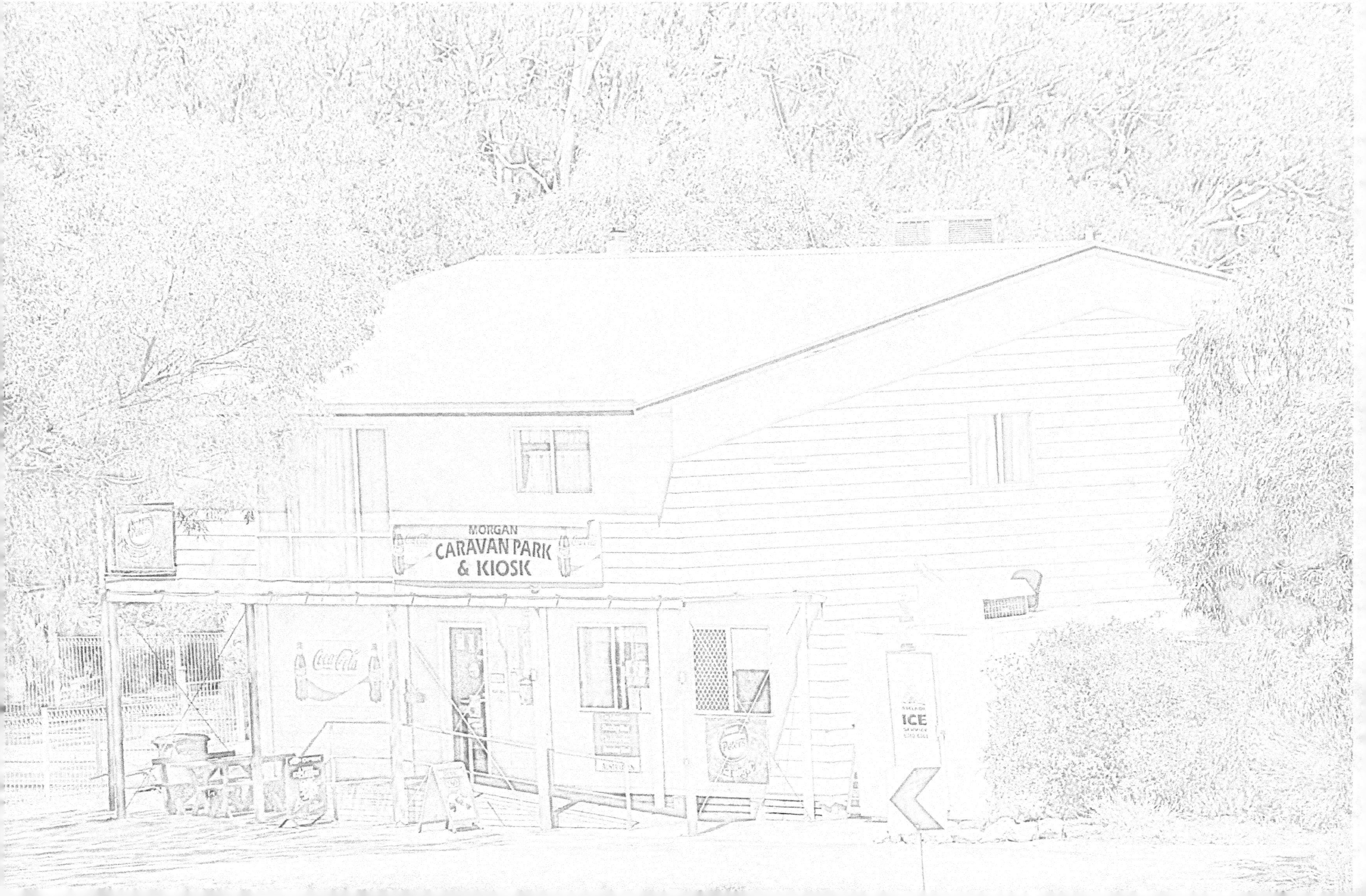
MORGAN
CARAVAN PARK
& KIOSK
Coca-Cola
ICE

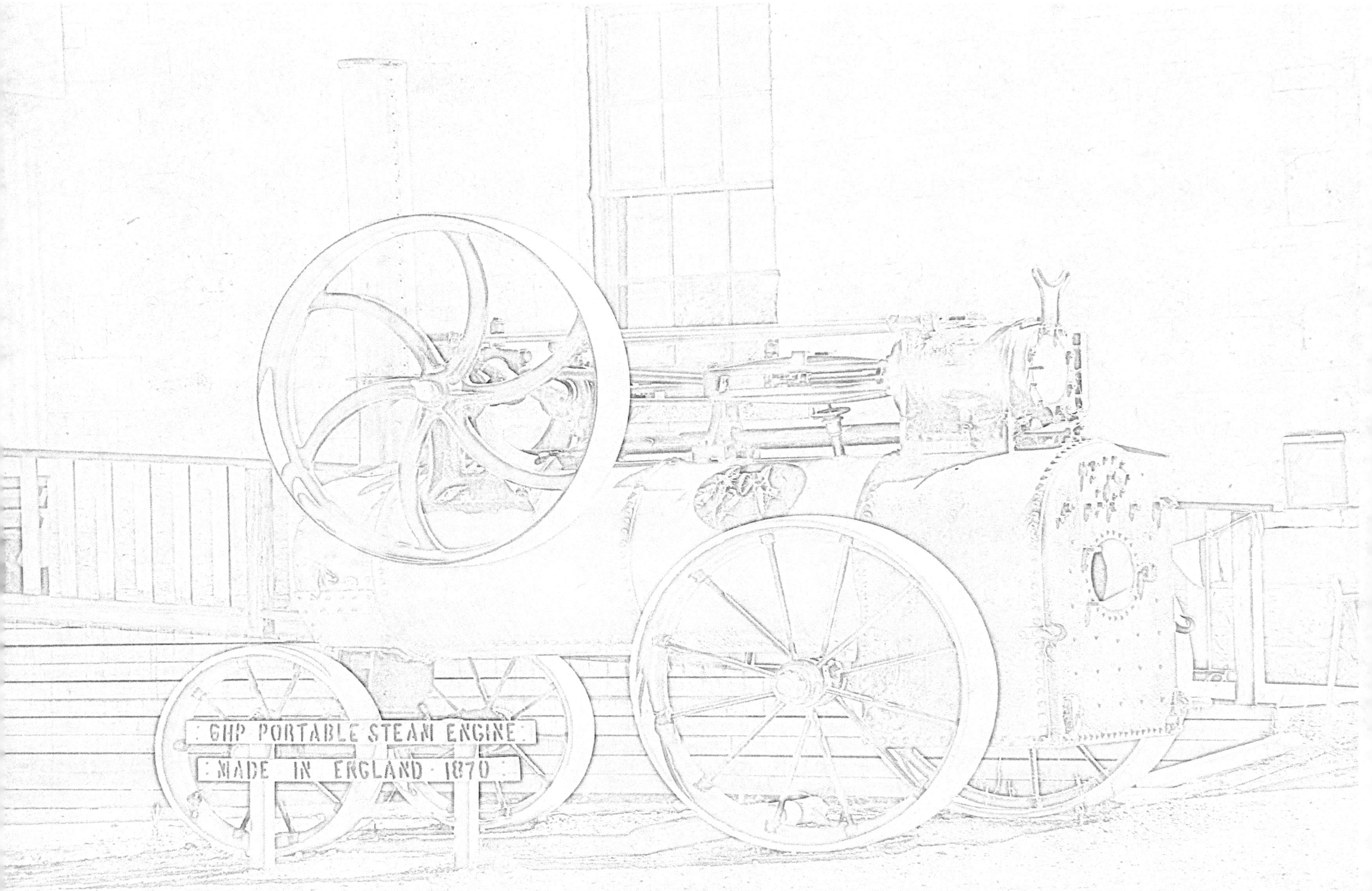
GHP PORTABLE STEAM ENGINE
MADE IN ENGLAND · 1870

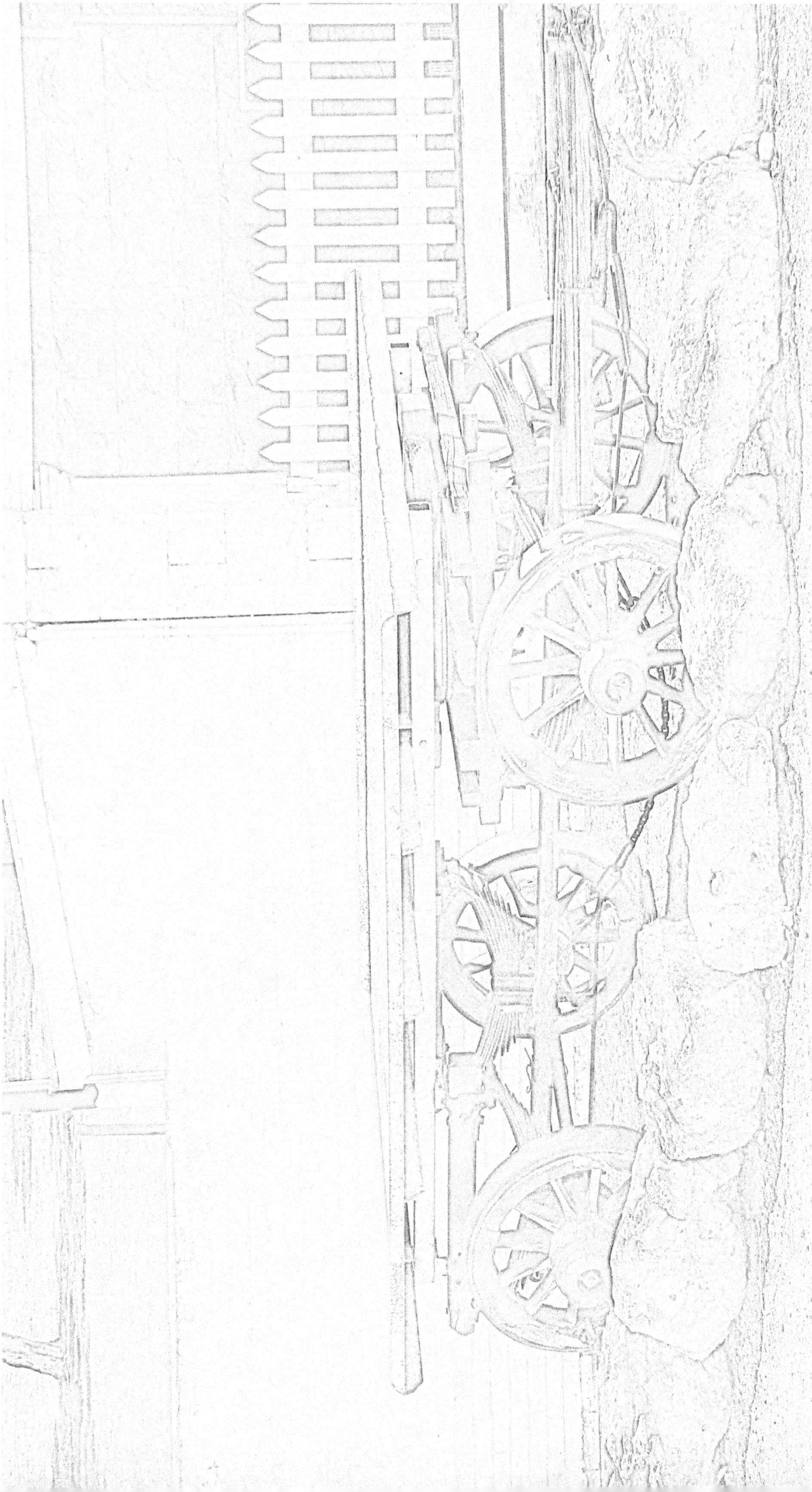

DREW &
CREWES
BUILDING
EST. 1902
saltbush
Ready For Anything

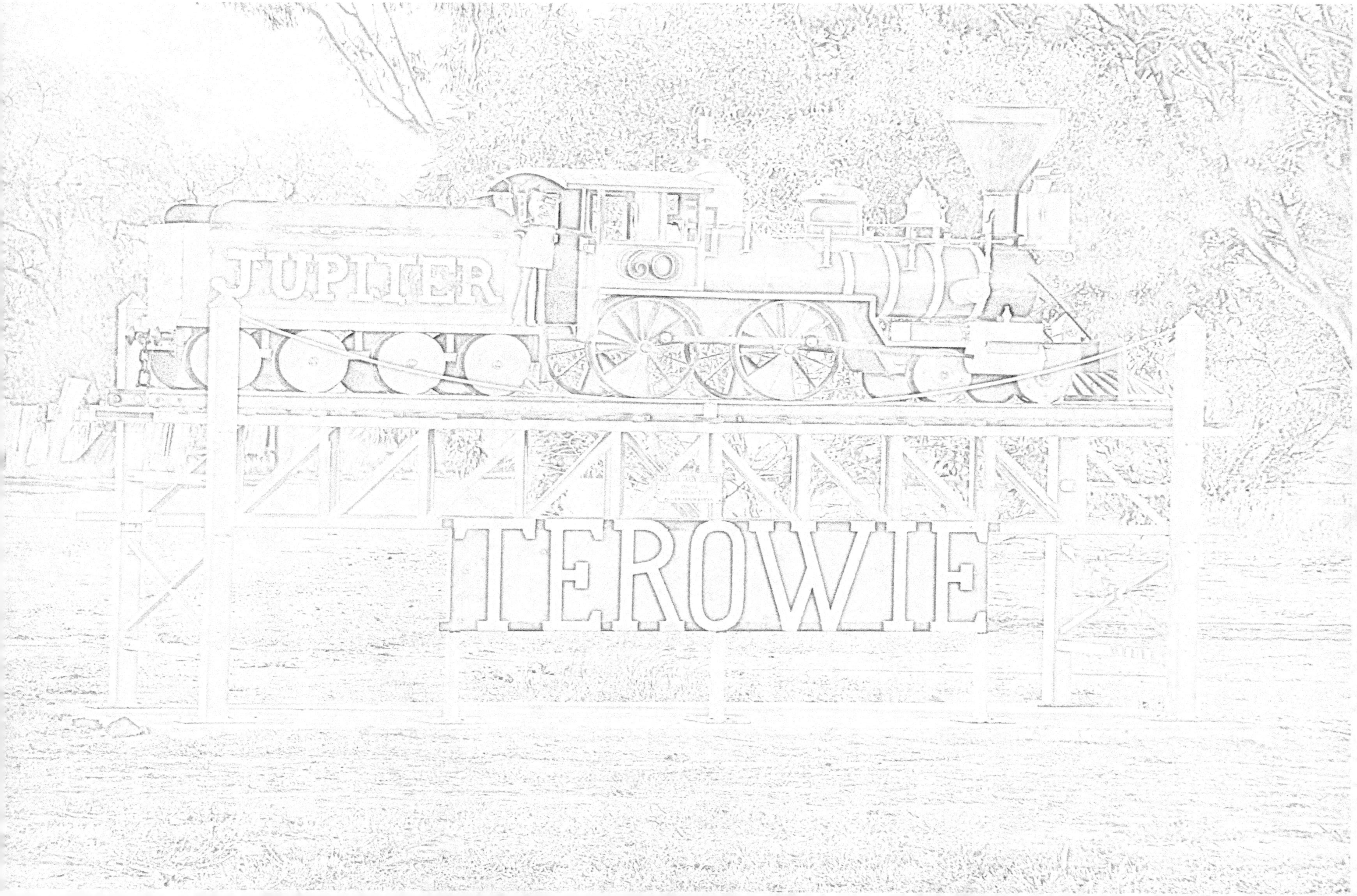
JUPITER
60
TEROWIE

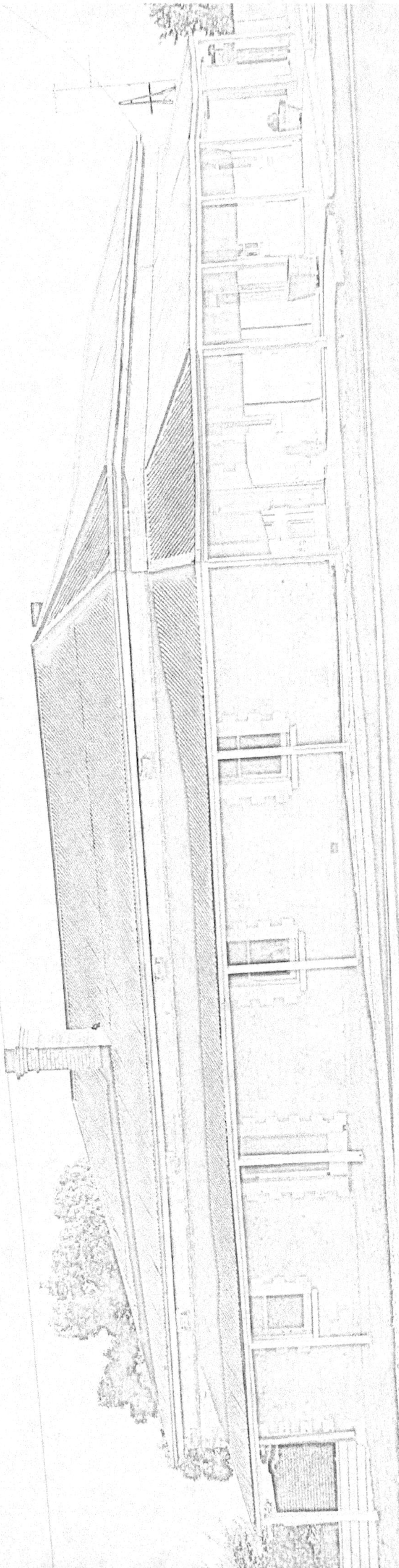

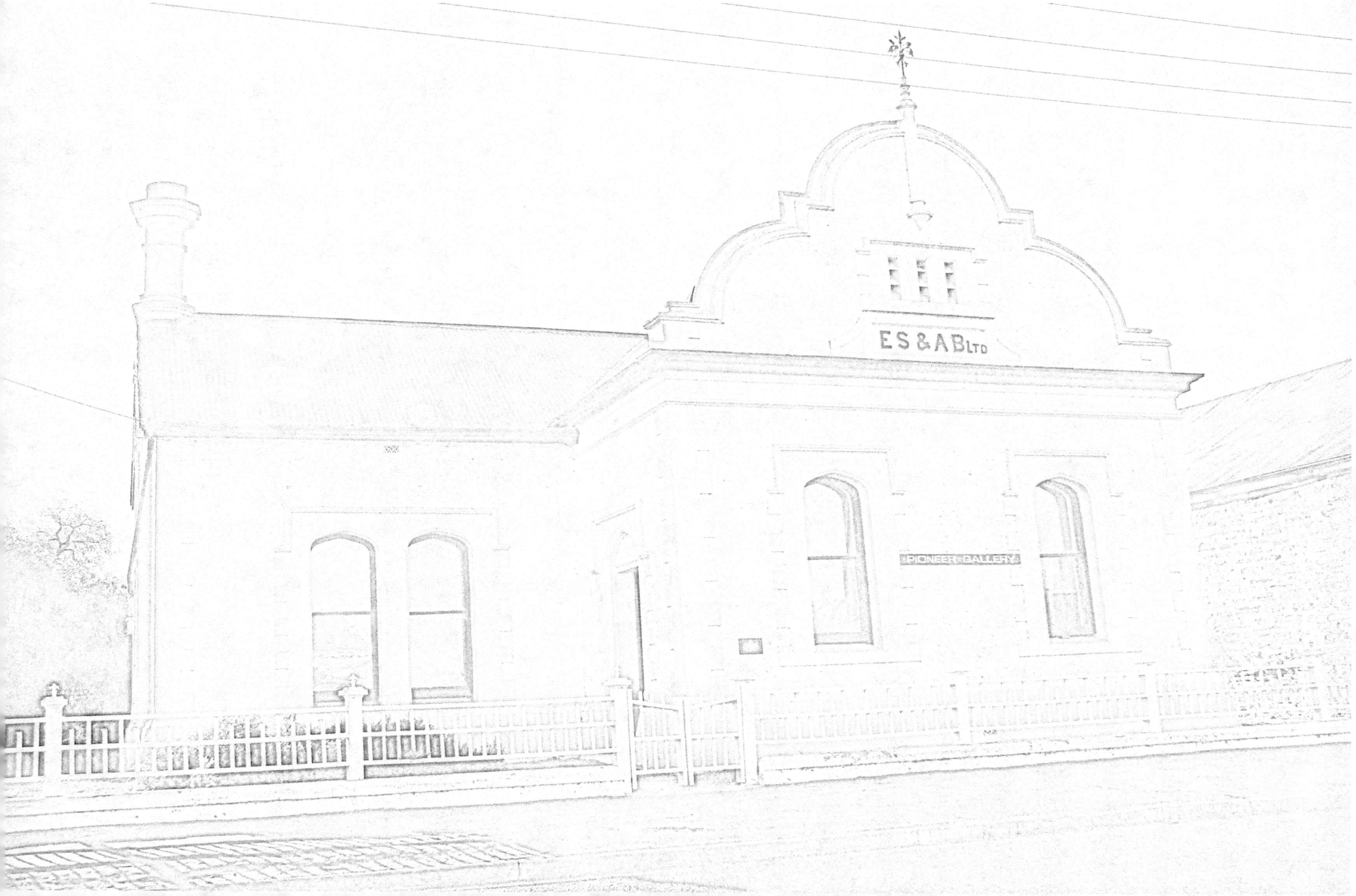
ES & AB LTD
PIONEER GALLERY

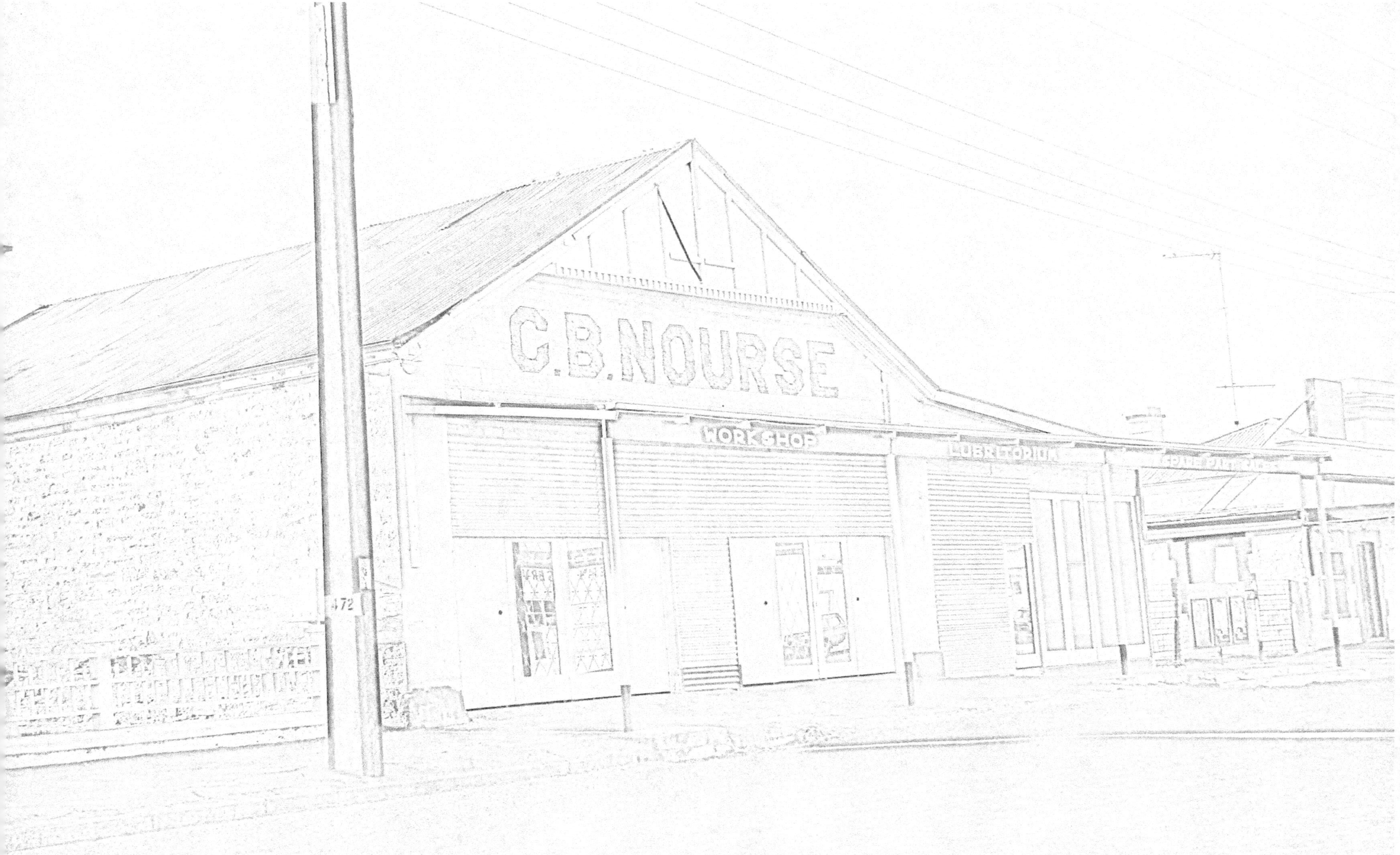
C.B.NOURSE
WORKSHOP
LUBRITORIUM
472

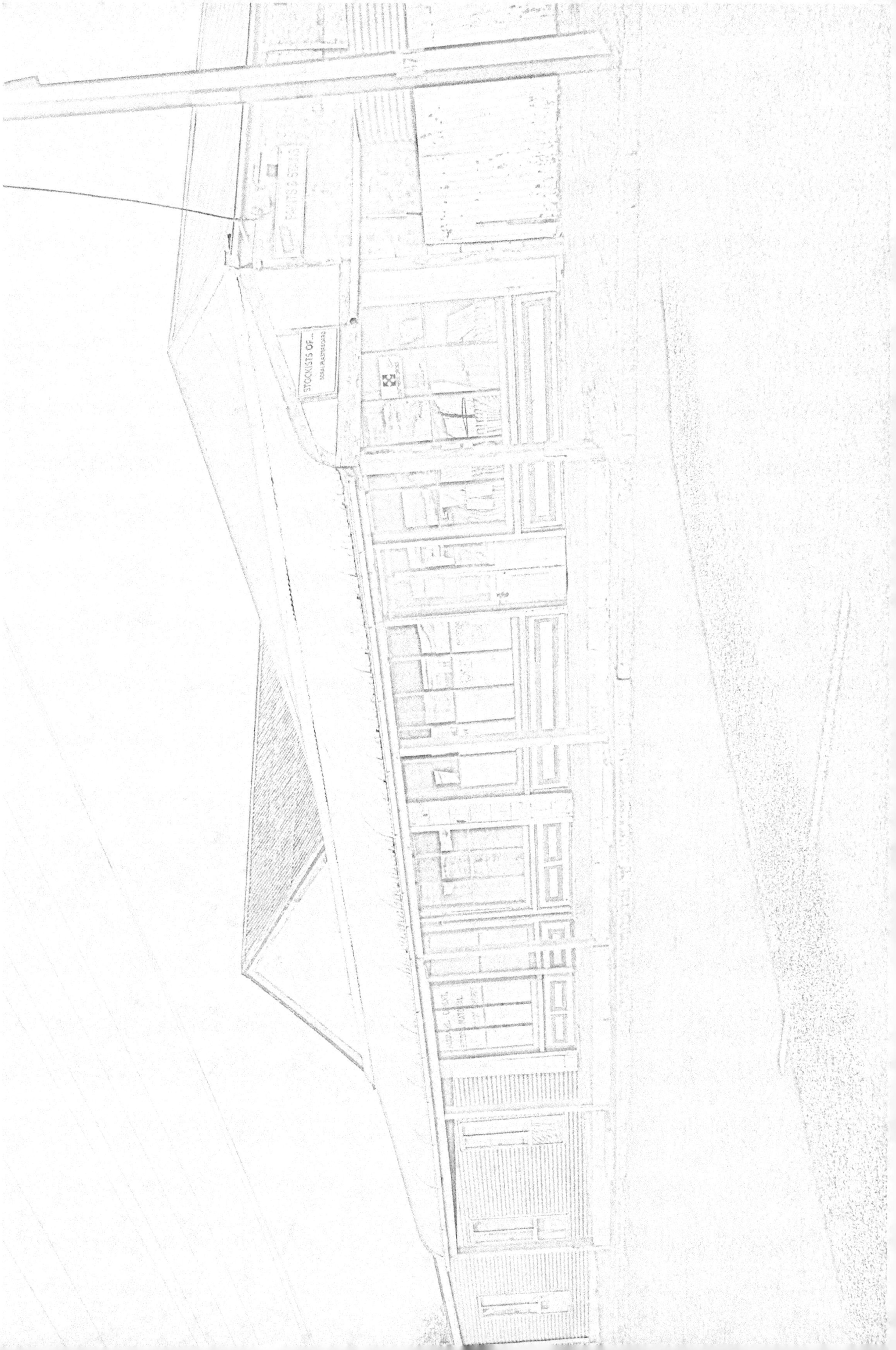
STOCKISTS OF...

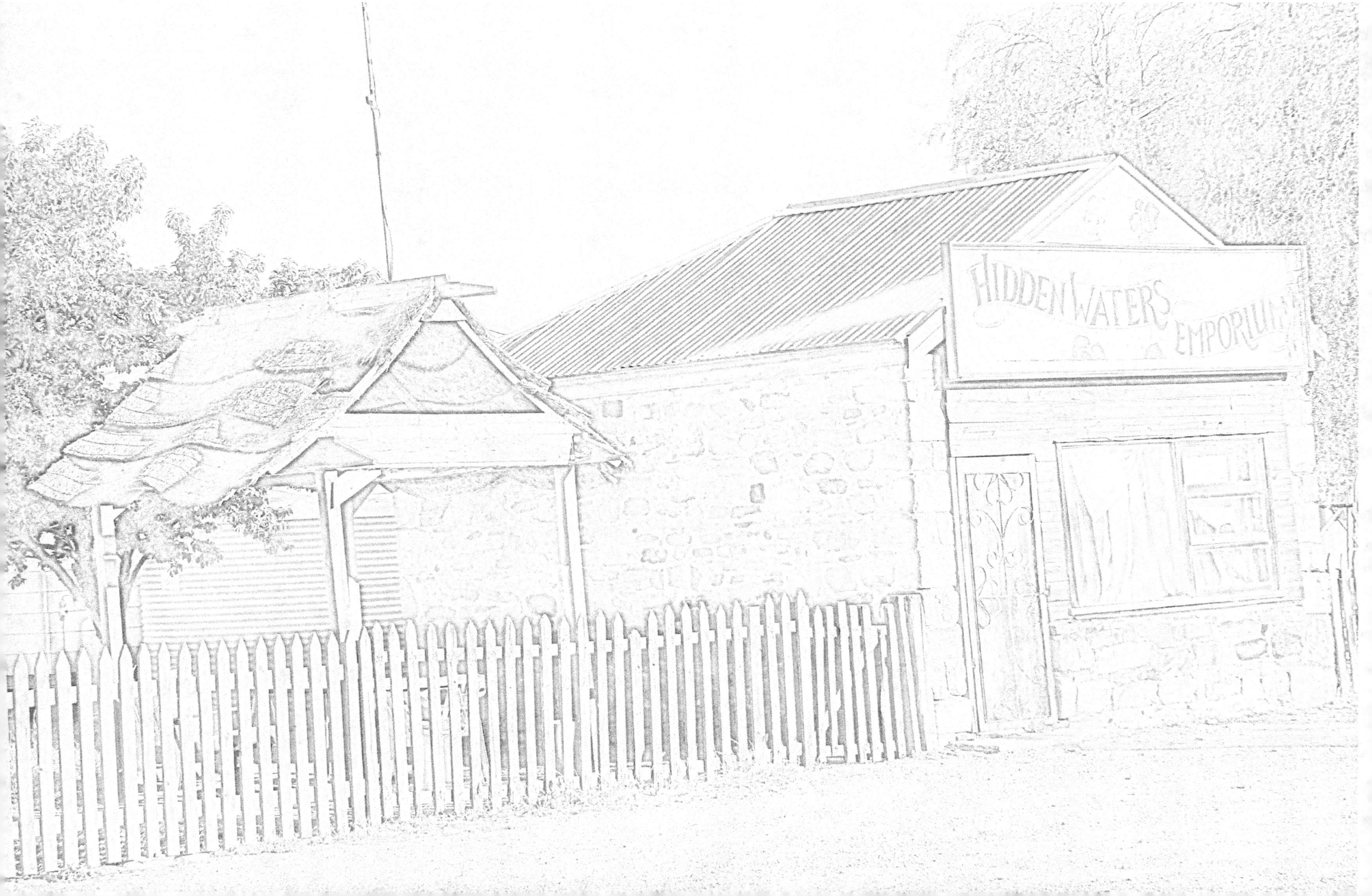
HIDDEN WATERS
EMPORIUM

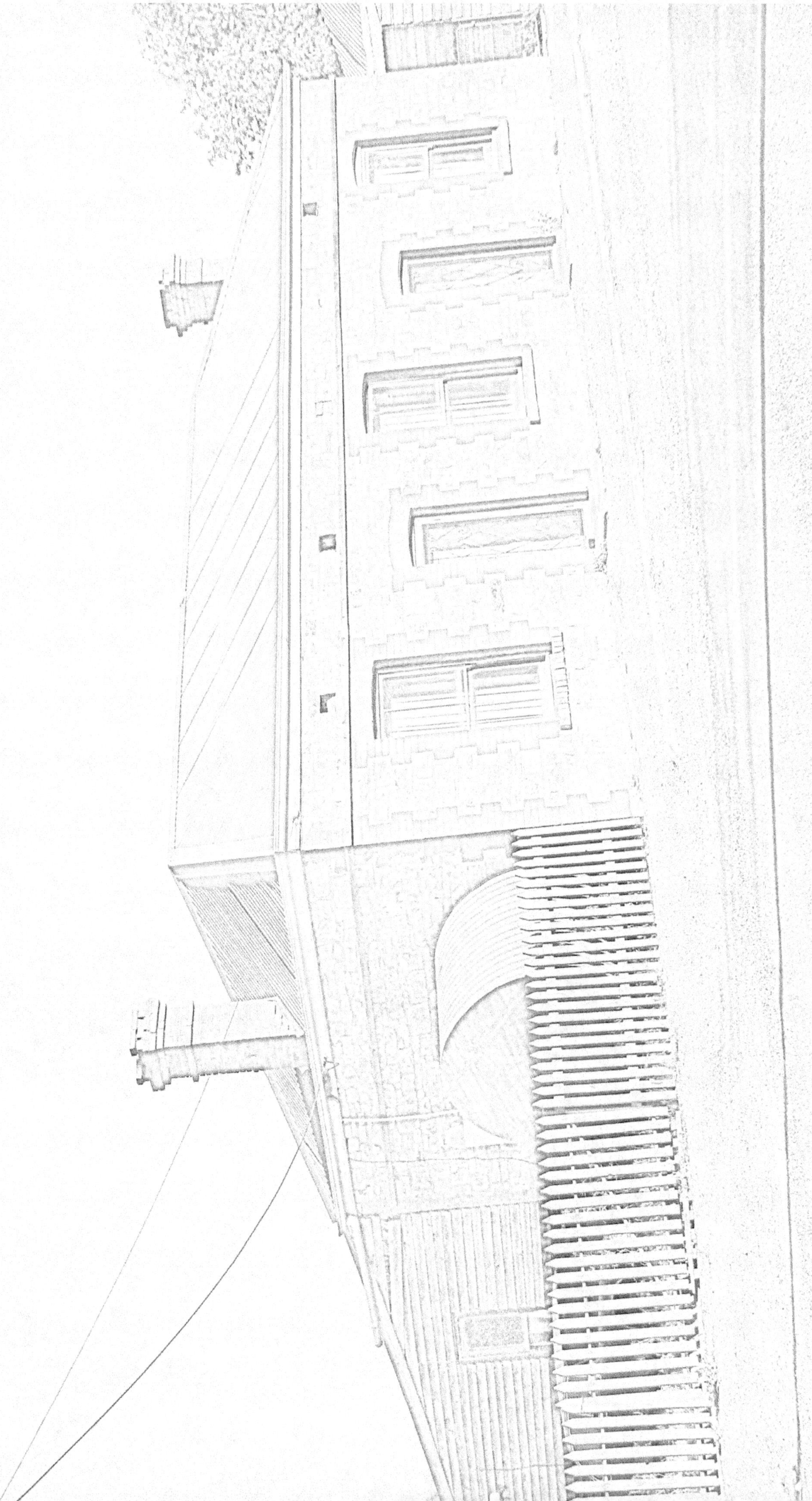

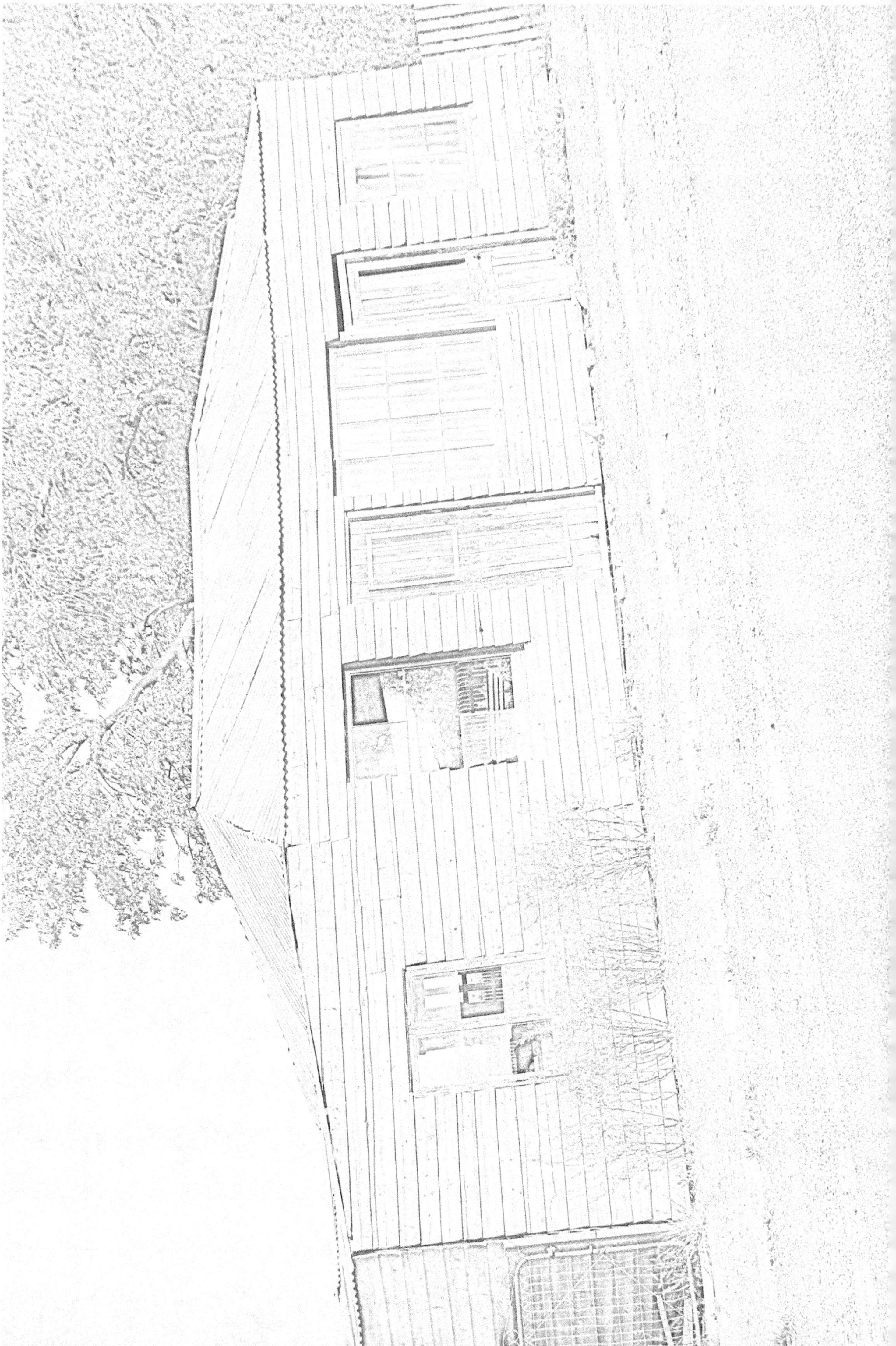

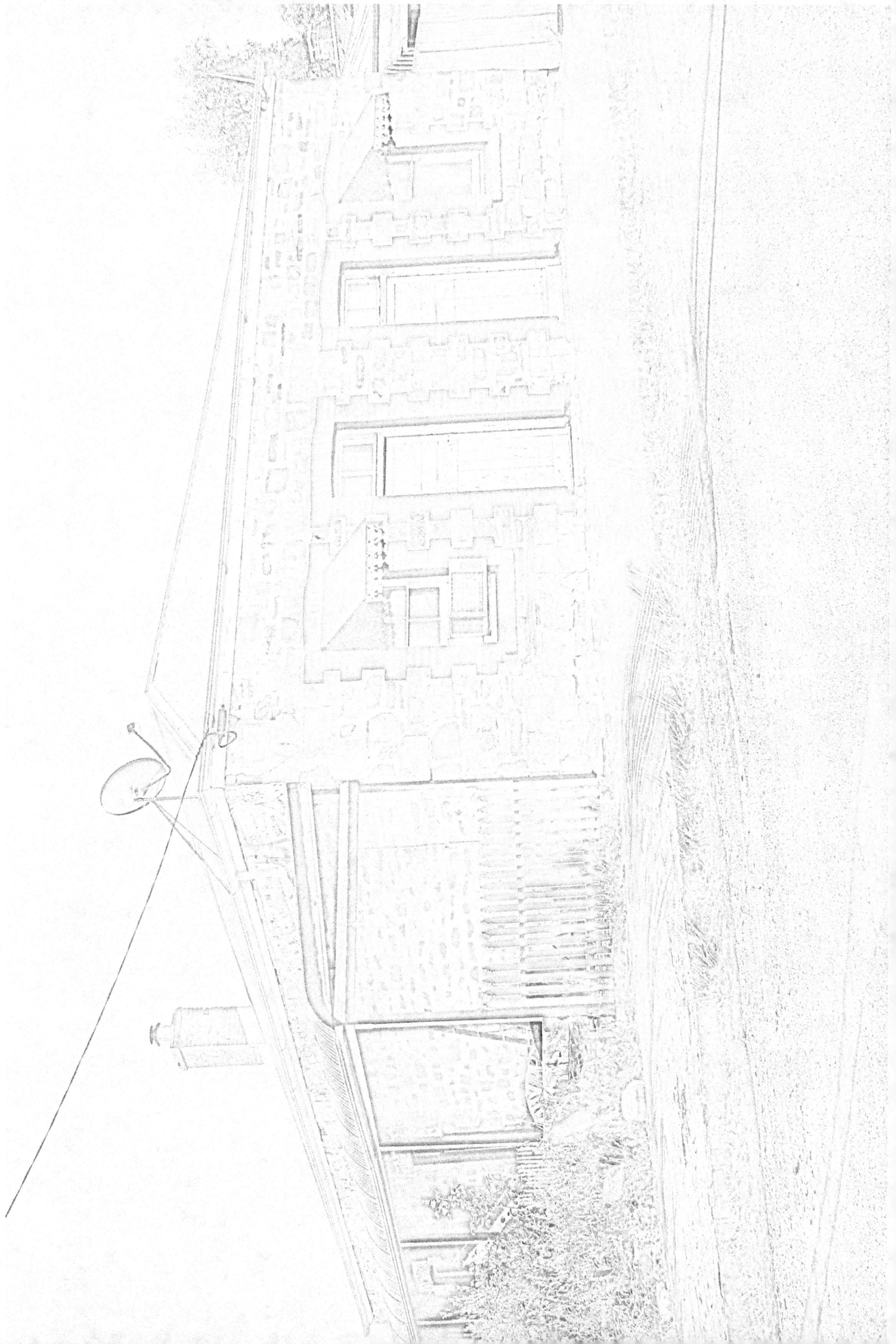

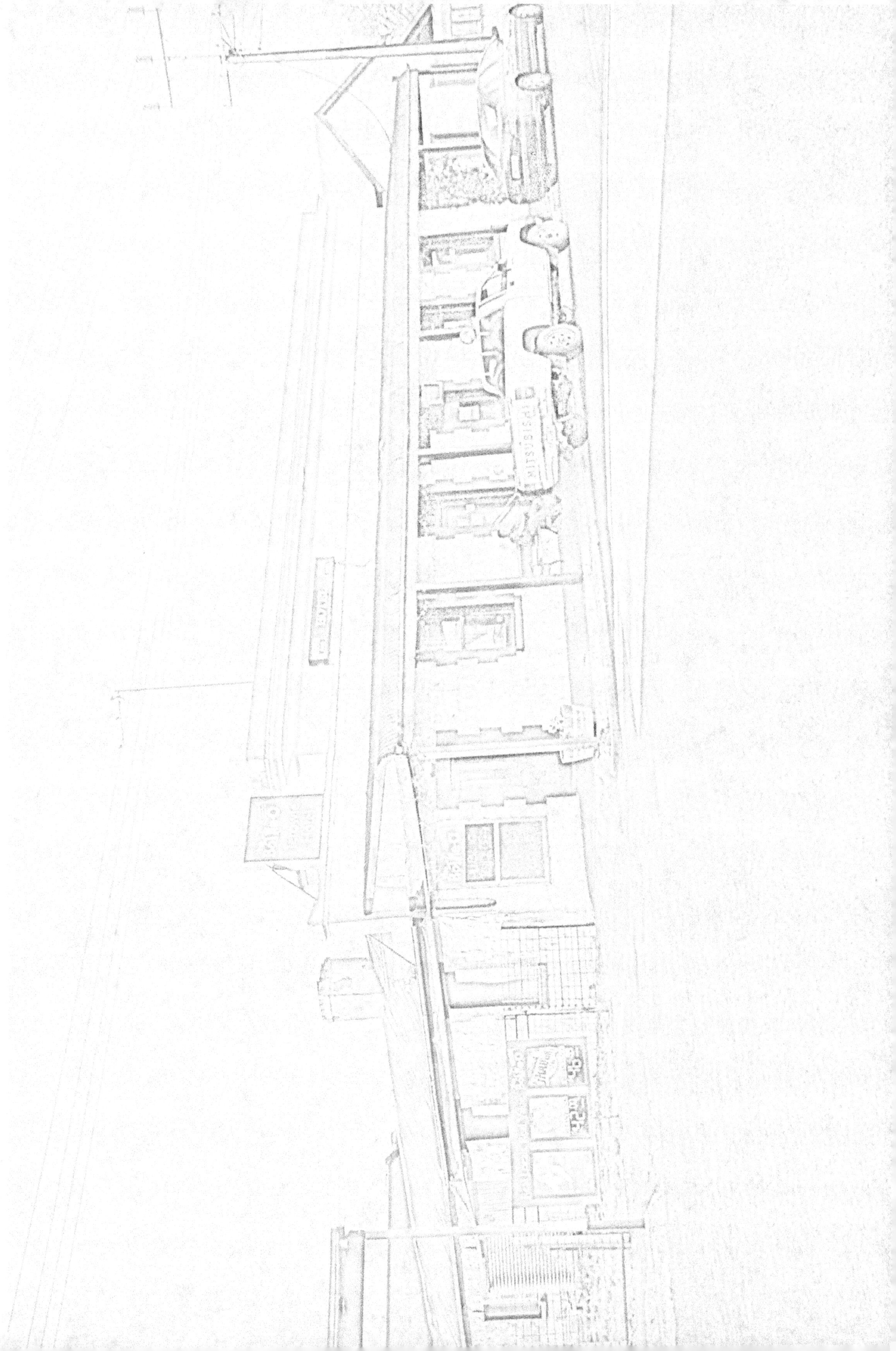

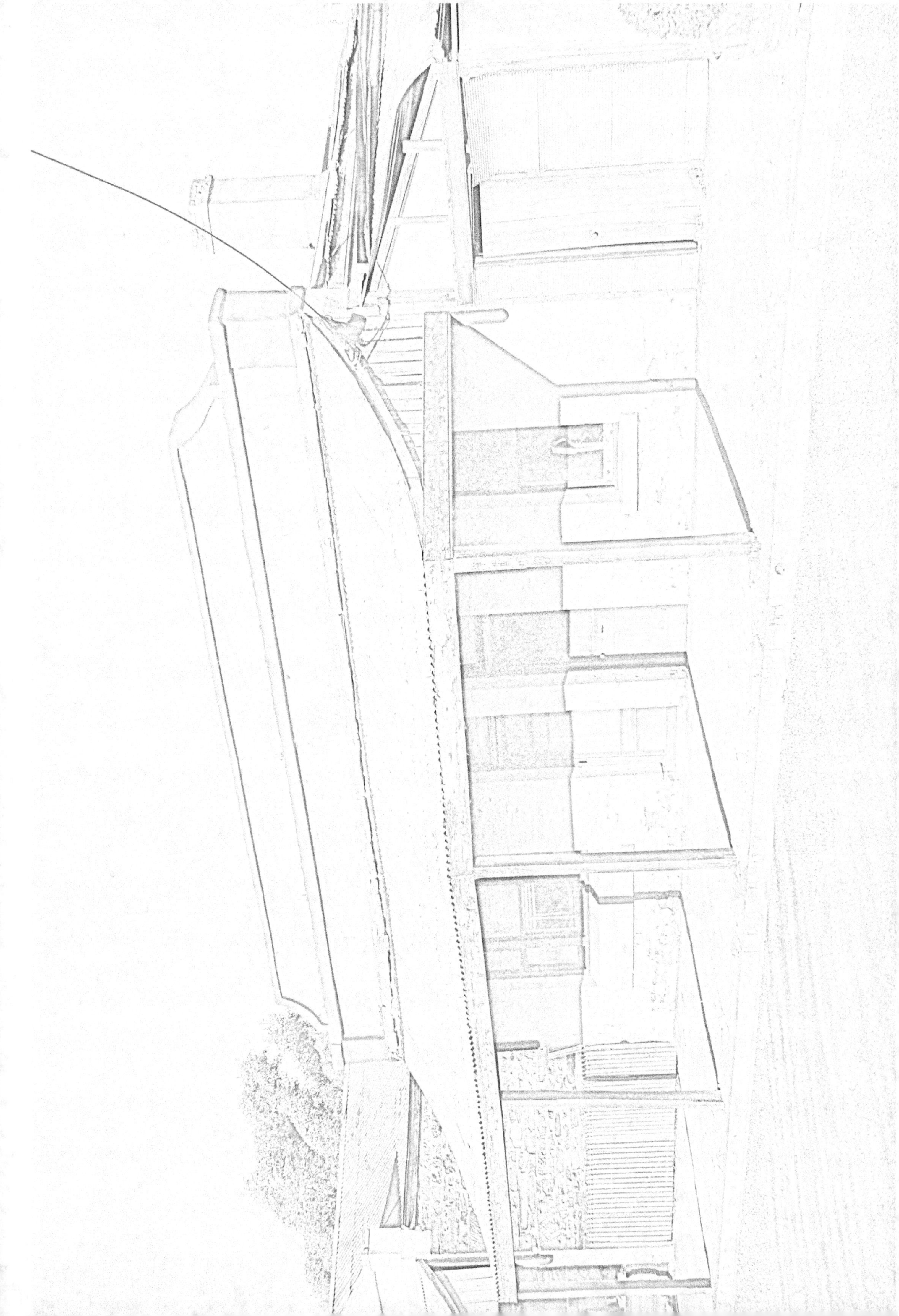

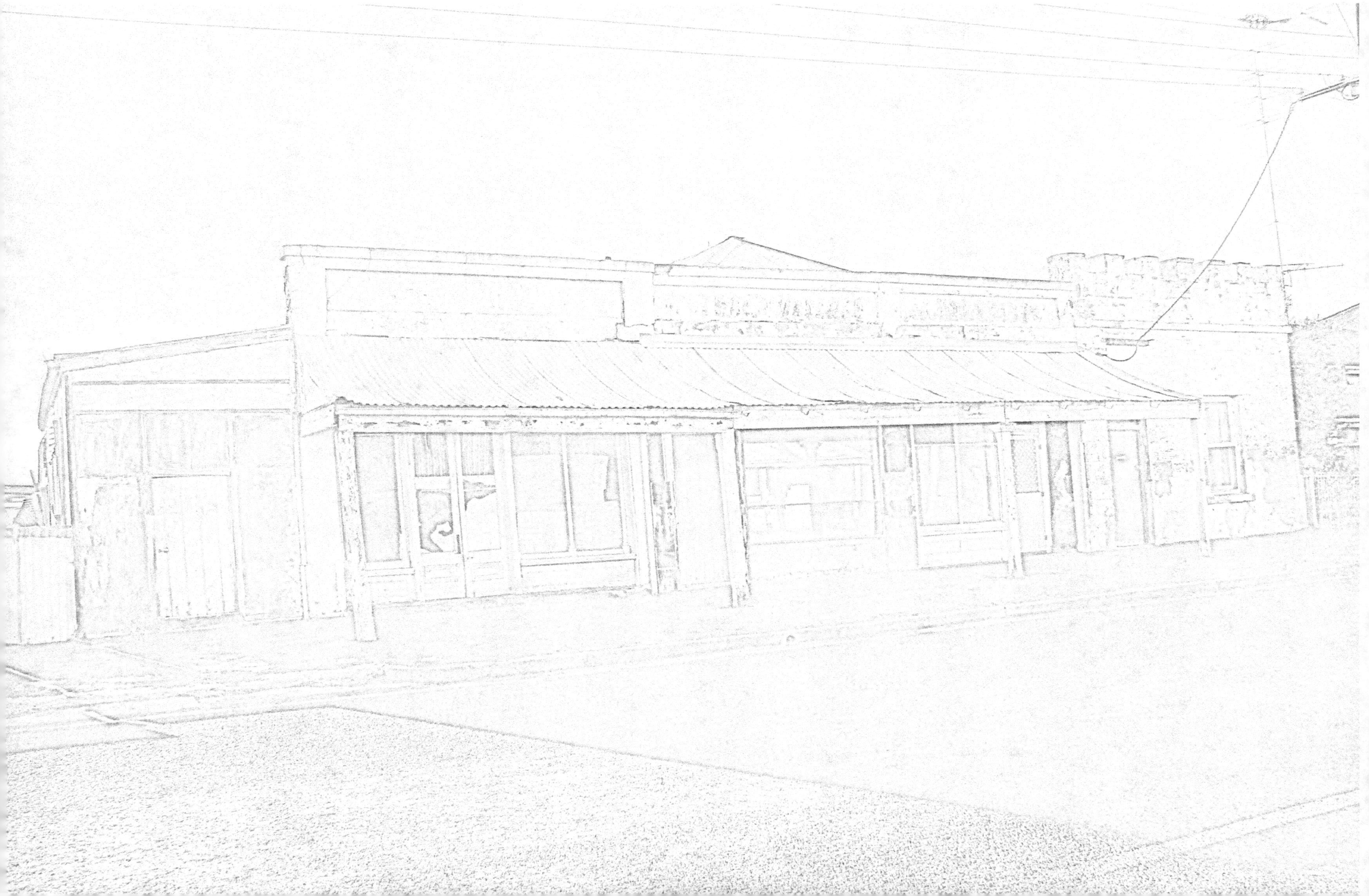

474

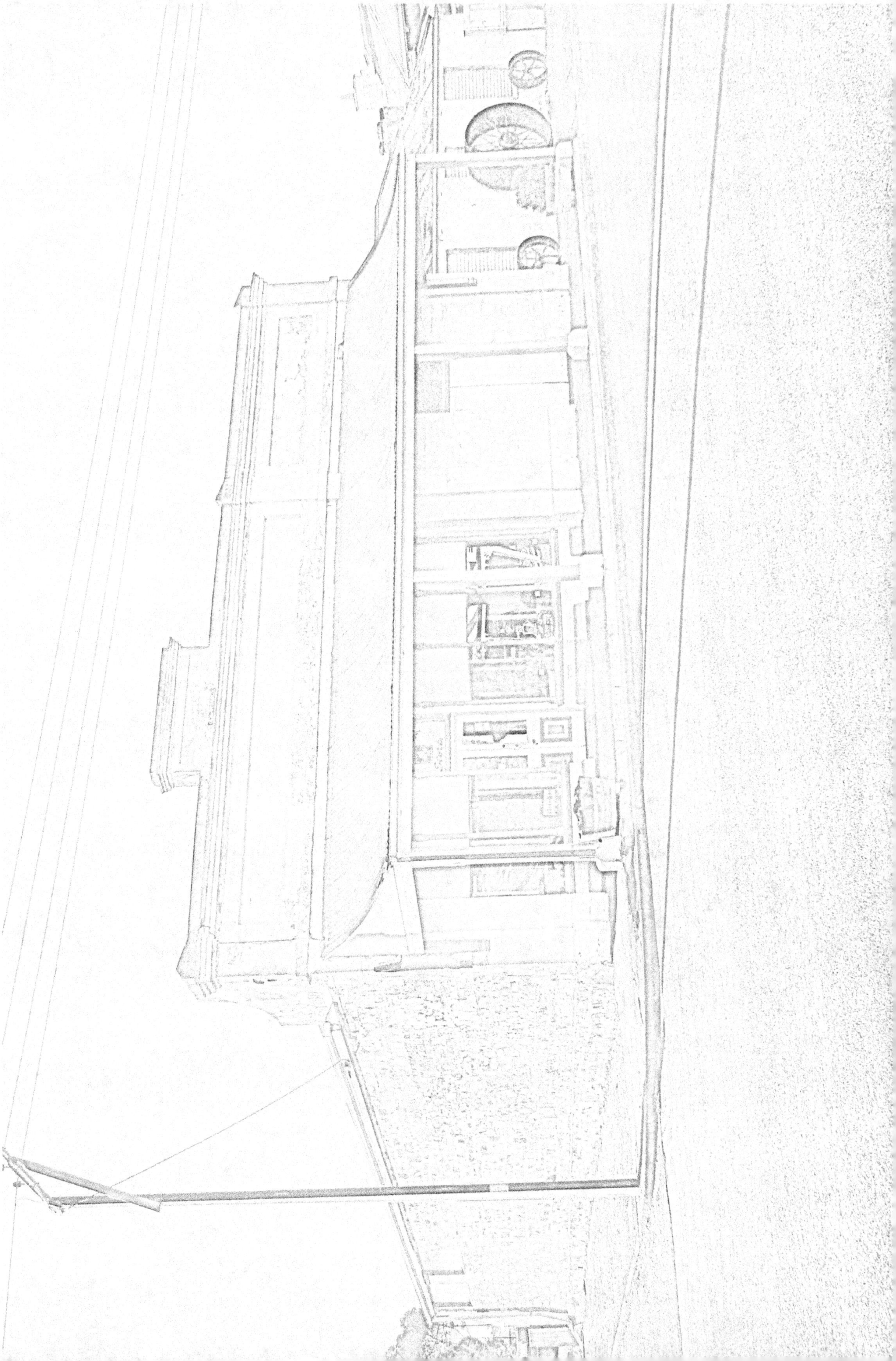

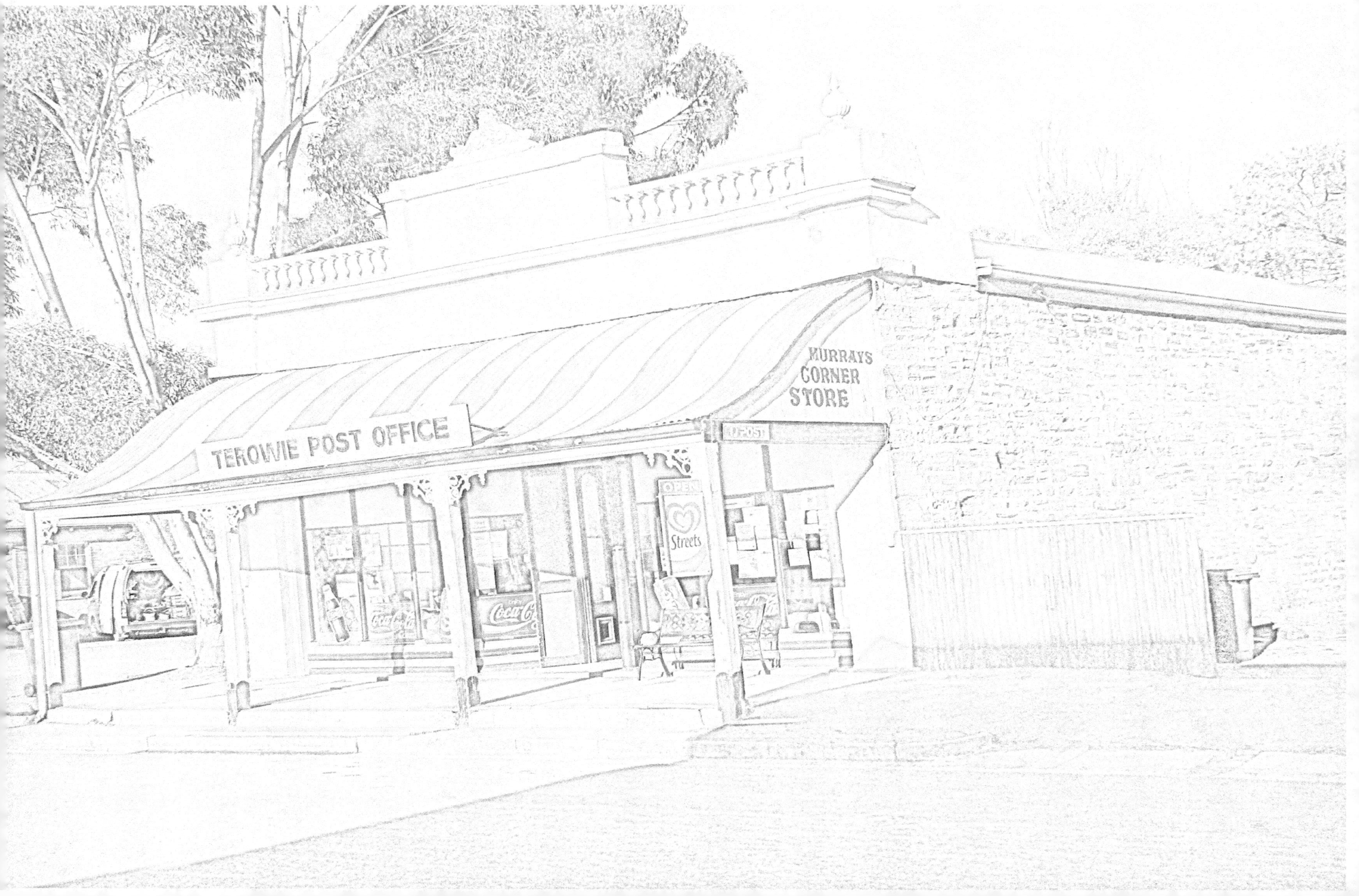
TEROWIE POST OFFICE
MURRAYS
CORNER
STORE
OPEN
Streets
Coca-Cola

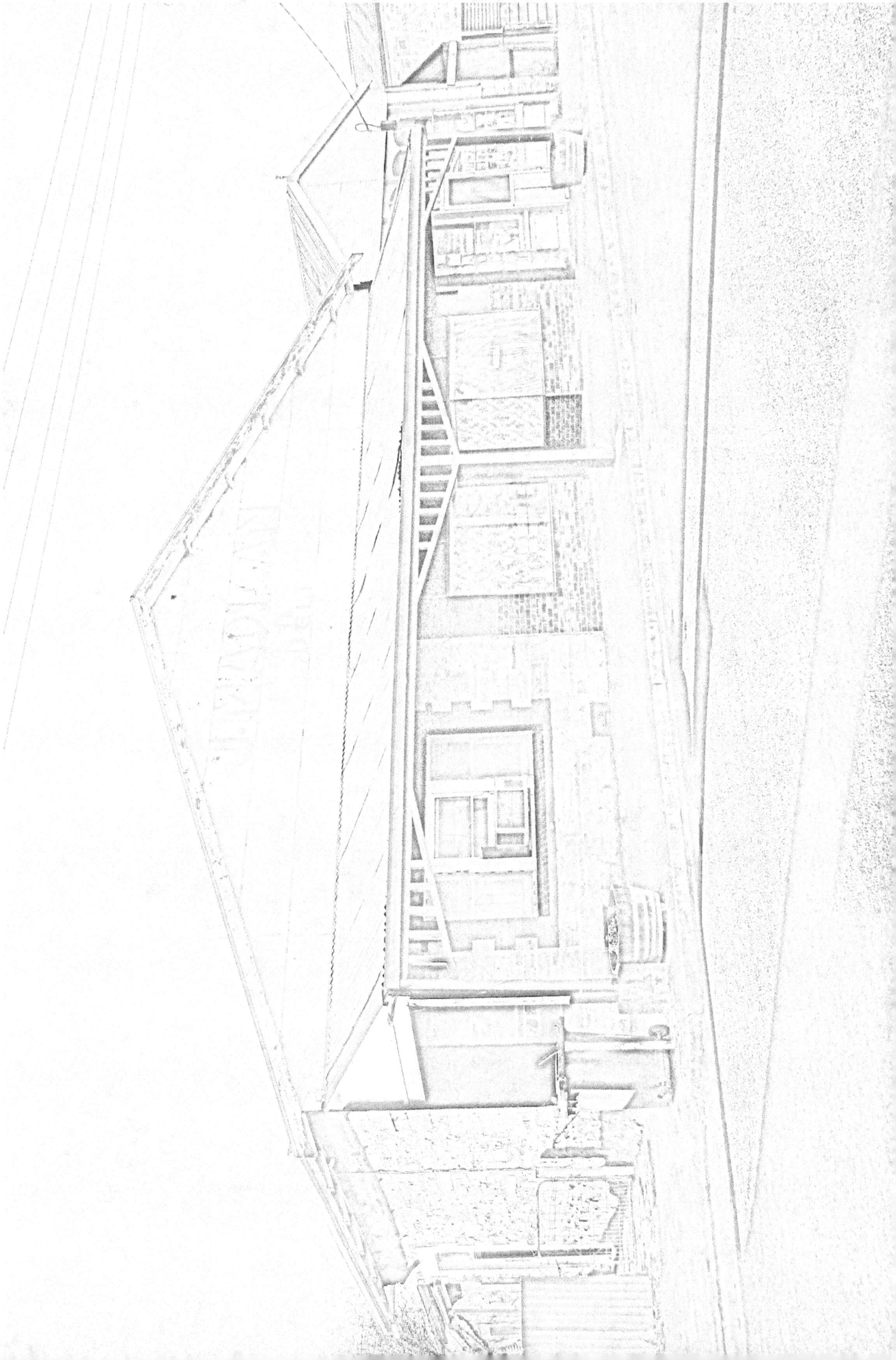

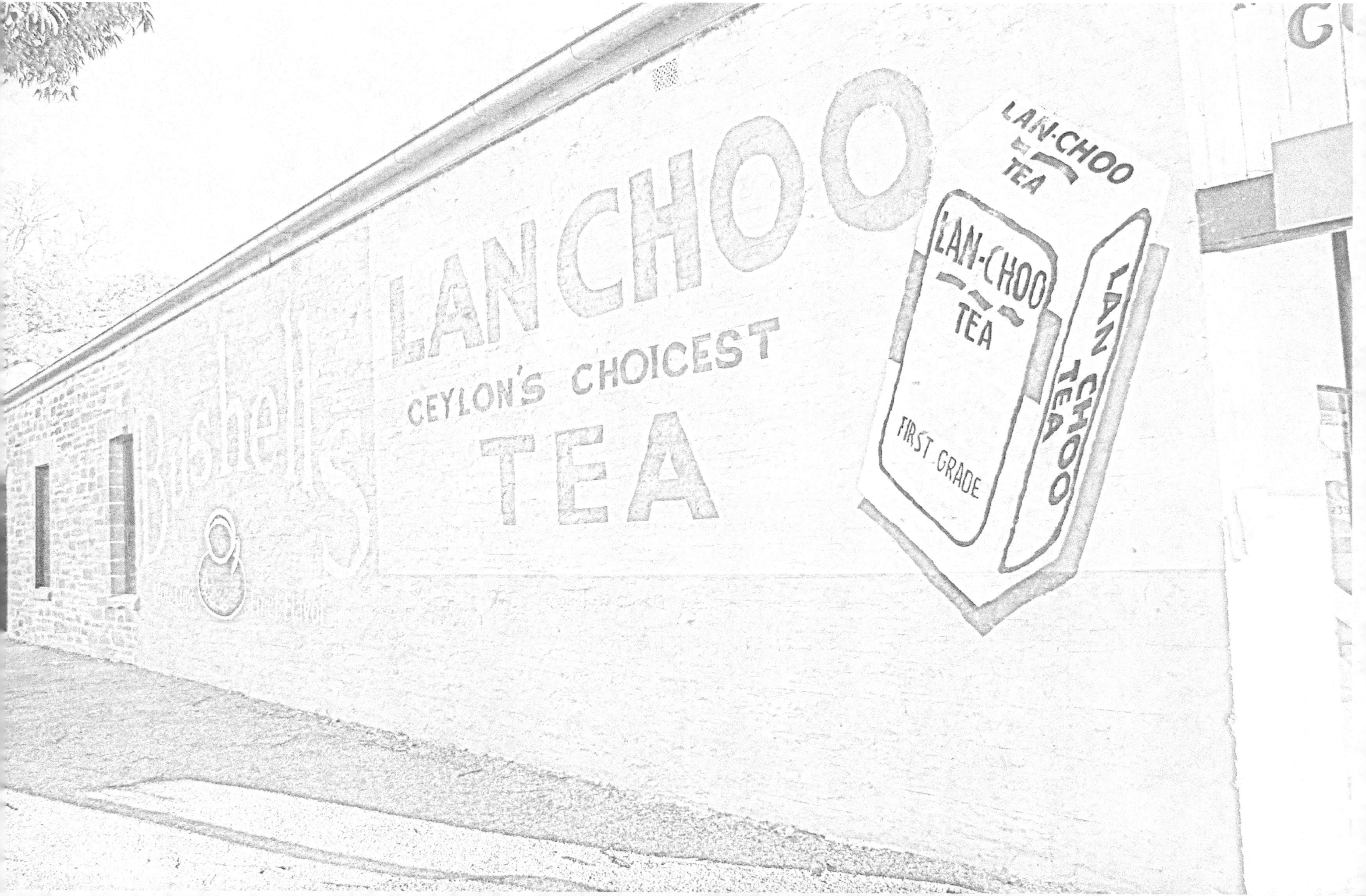
LAN CHOO
CEYLON'S CHOICEST
TEA
LAN-CHOO TEA
LAN-CHOO TEA
FIRST GRADE
LAN CHOO TEA
Bushells

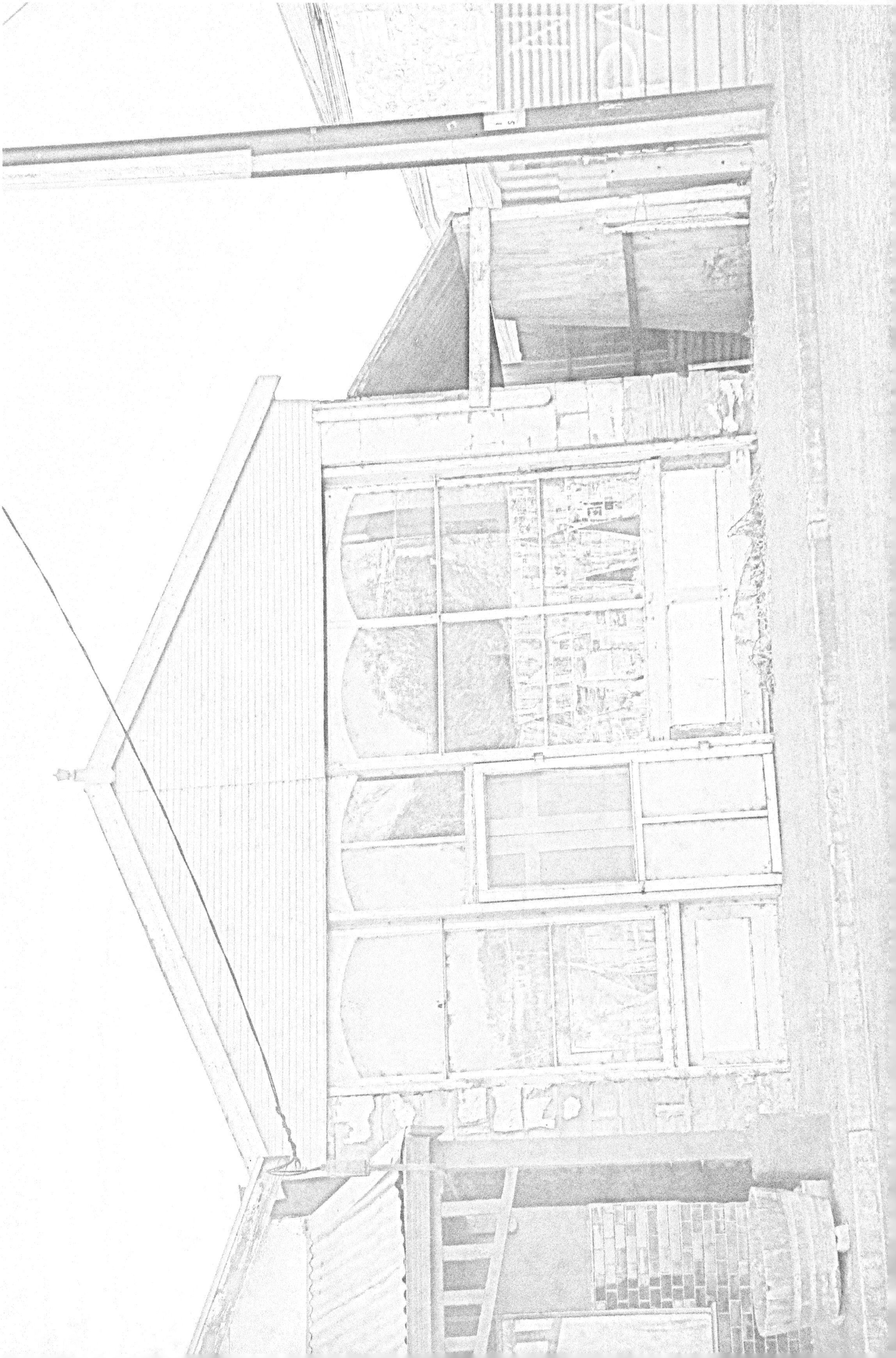

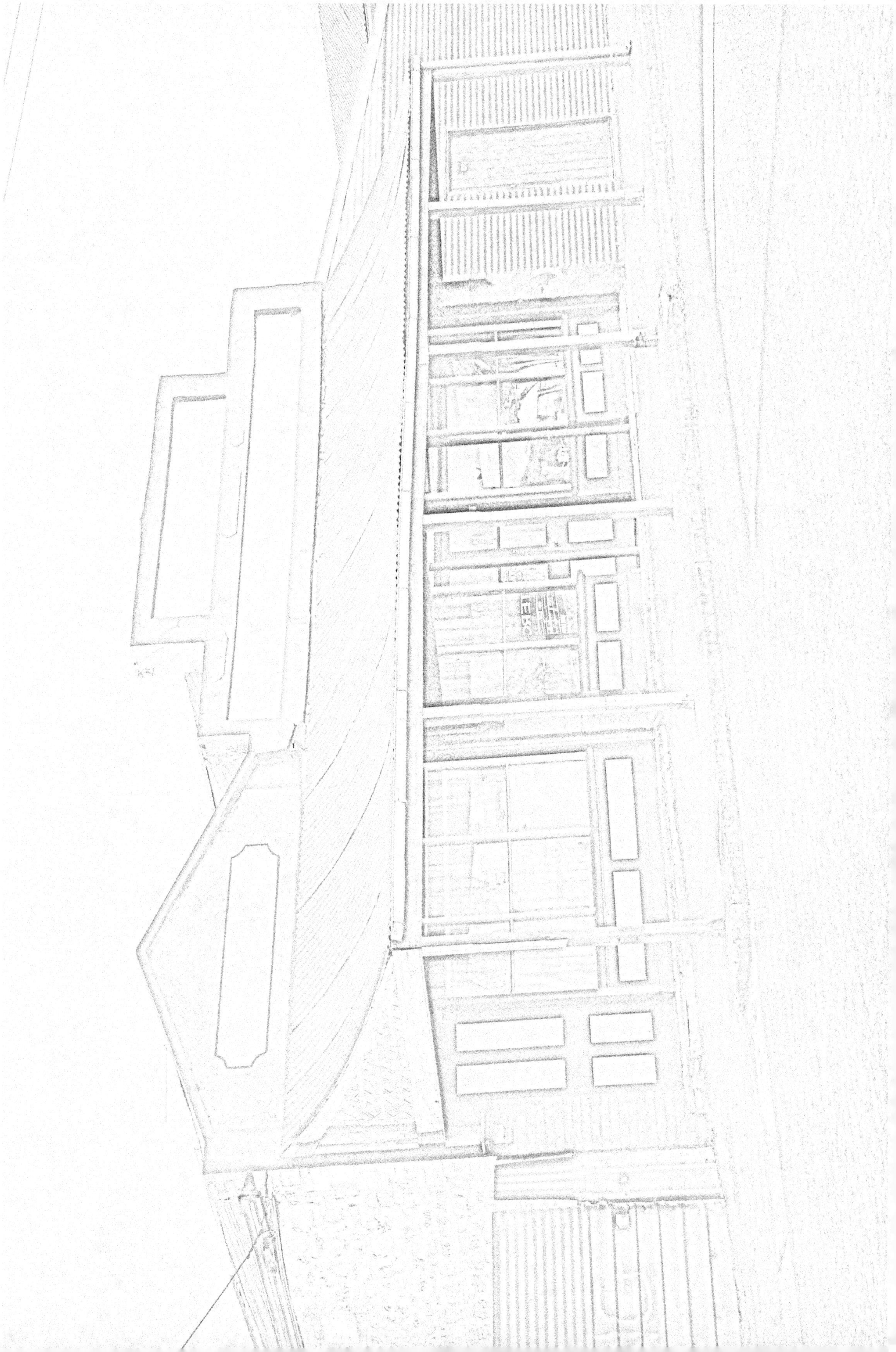

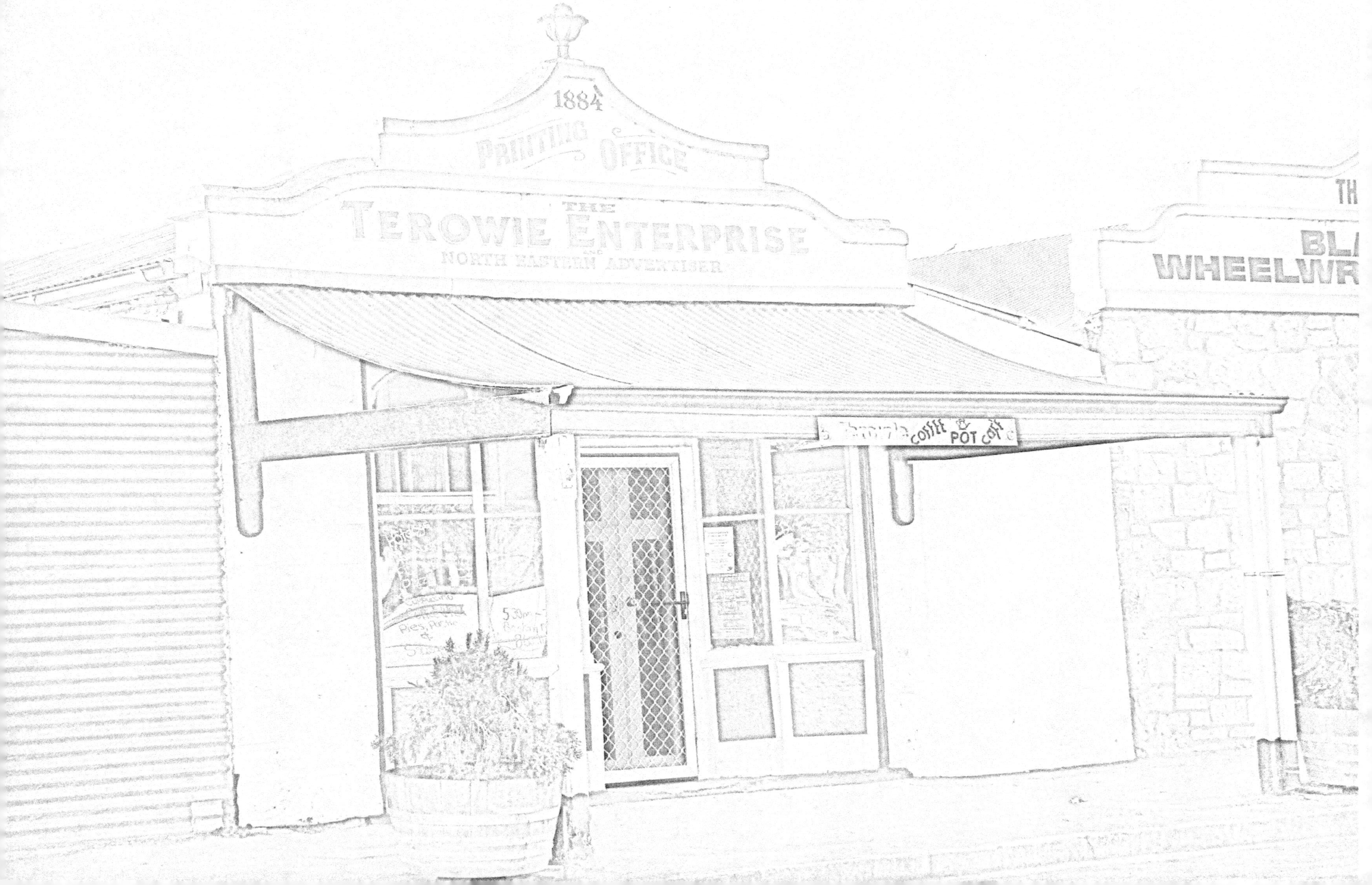
1884
PRINTING OFFICE
THE
TEROWIE ENTERPRISE
AND
NORTH EASTERN ADVERTISER
POT
WHEELWR

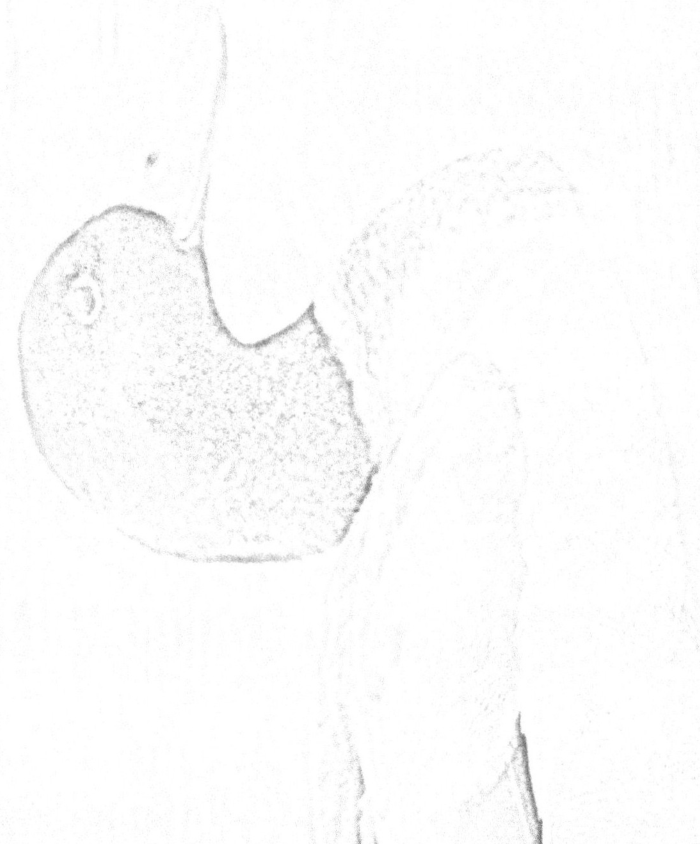

www.ingramcontent.com/pod-product-compliance
Lightning Source LLC
Chambersburg PA
CBHW081059180526
45170CB00005B/1818
* 9 7 8 0 3 5 9 9 7 2 0 9 8 *